Memory Lane

LEEDS

ALLEN ROWLEY retired in June 1992 as Promotions and Publicity Manager of Yorkshire Post Newspapers Ltd, after 50 years in the newspaper industry, starting out as a delivery boy.

'Retired', he says is something of a joke word, because after a brief period to get his typewriter 'revved-up' (along with one or two former colleagues like Keith Waterhouse, of the *Daily Mail*, he scorns word-processors and 'gizmos' and reckons he can work four times as fast with an ordinary typewriter), he went back to writing, mainly about trains and planes which are his favourite subjects, but also anything else that takes his fancy.

Following *Memory Lane Leeds 1* he wrote *Classic Steam*, which features pictures from the Yorkshire Post Newspapers 'Yorkshire Steam Collection' of photographs from the golden era of steam on British railways and then *Memory Lane Leeds – A Second Look*. When not engaged on those tasks he launched, compiled and edited Portraits of Steam, a highly popular *Yorkshire Post* quarterly publication for rail enthusiasts. He has also done public relations' consultancy work for Leeds Bradford International Airport and produced various publications in support of that task. He also writes on aviation matters for various magazines.

YORKSH RE
Evening Post

Memory Lane

LEEDS

DB
PUBLISHING

First published in Great Britain by The Breedon Books Publishing Company Limited Breedon House, 44 Friar Gate, Derby, DE1 1DA. 1996

Paperback edition published in Great Britain in 2011 by The Derby Books Publishing Company Limited, 3 The Parker Centre, Mansfield Road, Derby DE21 4SZ.

ISBN 978-1-85983-931-7

Printed and bound by Melita Press, Malta

Contents

ACKNOWLEDGEMENTS

In compiling this book the author received considerable assistance from the following staff of *Yorkshire Post* Newspapers: Mrs Anne McQueen, Chief Librarian; Miss Jayne Marsden, Deputy Chief Librarian; Mrs Jane Tansey, Photographic Administrator; Miss Vicky Linley, Photographic Receptionist. He also records his particular thanks to his wife, Joyce, for her valuable research, and for her patience.

The majority of pictures in this book are from the Library or Photographic Department of *Yorkshire Post* Newspapers, and the publishers are grateful for permission to use them. Sources of other pictures are acknowledged in the captions.

LEEDS – AN INTRODUCTION

Until Leeds almost leapt into the headlines as a financial centre which was attracting national and international businesses in considerable numbers – all within the last 25 years – it was not unusual to talk with visitors to the city from the South of England and fins that two fallacies would soon emerge: firstly, that during the Victorian period the city 'sprang up' as if from nowhere; secondly, nothing of note happened in Leeds before that time.

It came as a surprise to such visitors to learn that less than a mile beyond the city's present northern boundary, there was once a Roman camp. In fact, Romans spent a good deal of time tramping their version of the super highway 'twixt' York and Ilkley, to use a word beloved of estate agents.

And at Adel, not far across the fields from that camp site, the original Saxon church was replaced around 1150 by the present structure which has a much-admired specimen of Norman architecture amd design in the shape of its doorway.

Most records of the city's history lean to the theory that it had Roman origins. Its very name is said to have come down from a Roman or Brigantian description for a 'town in the forest'. This seems likely, for long after the Romans left, huge swathes of Broad Acres were covered by trees.

Granted, it was much slower than York to come to prominence and poll tax records of 1378 show that Leeds was of less importance than Pontefract, which had a larger population and consequently paid more tax. Sheffield, Wakefield, Selby, Snaith and Ripon also paid more than Leeds, whose bill came to £3 0s 4d, there being only 50 families to tax. Some 100 years later, Leeds was recorded as 'being near Rothwell'.

It is true that the 14th and 15th centuries did not bring development in Leeds of great interest to national scribes and later historians, although there was plenty going on in the area – especially aming Yorkists and Lancastrians. But an important visitor in 1536 was not too impressed and delivered what would have been the crowning insult, and no doubt have raised residents to fury had it been said centuries later, when he declared that Leeds was not as 'quick' (enterprising) as Bradford.

A matter of opinion, for men of the cloth – the woven variety – driven out of York by practices they felt did not act in their favour, were setting up their businesses in Leeds and found the place most accomodating.

It seems clear, therefore, that the citizens of Leeds in those times were already well-tuned to an attitude that would see the city grow rapidly in the 18th and 19th centuries: minding their own business which is, perhaps, from where another well-know expression sprang.

Galloping around the countryside between castles on horses 'covered in curtains' might have been all right for the landed gentry and knights of old; but the entrepeneurs of Leeds saw more sense and a better future in cloth to cover the ever-increasing population, which had grown from 16,380 in 1771 to 30,669 by 1801. And th population of the West Riding as a whole more than doubled between 1841 and 1891.

That such a course was the right one was emphasised by the middle of the 16th century when the city had outstripped many of the surrounding towns in terms of size and importance. King Charles I gave Leeds its first Royal Charter (spelling it 'Leedes') in 1626, elevating it to the dignity of a municipal borough. It was, however, worded in such a way that the townsfolk had no voice in the management of their own affairs and the town was run by the Crown's nominees and subsequently their appointees.

The charter did give praise to the townsfolk for 'skilfully exercising the art and mystery of making and working woollen cloths', whose then common name was 'Northern Dozens'. One doubts that would have the same beneficial reference as the 'baker's dozen'!

Perhaps West Riding's oddly named shoddy trade had already made its start, for the charter also referred to 'diverse clothiers...who have begun to make deceptive cloths to everybody's harm and prejudice'.

The Civil War intruded upon these busy folk in 1643 and principal manufacturers sent a message to the King, then at York, begging him to make peace with Parliament. He took no heed and Leeds

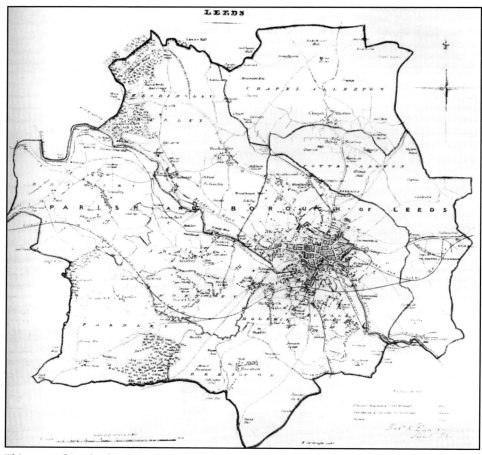

This map of Leeds, dated 1832, was made by Lieutenant Robert K. Dawson, Royal Engineers. It clearly shows the proposed boundary of the Borough, and parish boundaries are also shown. The map was prepared in time for the Reform Act.

What is also clear is that the town did not simply grow outwards over the years, but a good deal of in-filling took place between the vilages and Hamlets around it; some of which were as old as Leeds itself; some even older.

At the time the map was made, the built-up area of the town was a little over a mile across and travellers were soon out into the countryside. Leeds stretched from roughly where the Yorkshire Television premises are today in the west to Burmantofts and Richmond Hill in the east; and from Holbeck Moor in the south to about halfway down North Street.

Chapel Allerton, Potter Newton, Hunslet, Beeston, Wortley, Armley, Kirkstall, Bramley, Headingley, Woodhouse and Buslingthorpe were simply villages or hamlets. There was a barracks, of which there are still traces, north-east of Sheepscar.

Street Lane, Gledhow, Gipton, Coldcotes, Halton Dial, Stourton, Farnley, Swinnow, Hawksworth Park and Meanwood Hall were out in the country. Cookridge was at the 'back of beyond...'

But things were on the move : the Leeds and Selby Railway line was in business, give or take a few yards; and the proposed line of the Bradford and Leeds Railway is shown. We are grateful to Mr Richard Hainsworth for supplying us with a copy of this map.

'Loiners', a name which appears throughout this publication, is the generally accepted term for people born in the city of Leeds.

was garrisoned on his behalf. Eventually, Sir Thomas Fairfax and a Parliamentary force marched on the city and from Woodhouse Moor sent a message to the Royalist commander, Sir William Savile, ordering him to surrender immediately.

He refused, and a battle commenced, especially around St John's Church, at the top of Briggate. The main battle, near Leeds Bridge, was won by Parliamentarians who were later overcome again and held until the Royalist cause was terminated in a bloody battle at Marston Moor, near Wetherby and York.

There were few Civil War casualities in Leeds, but in 1644 hundreds dies in an outbreak of plague. Within a few months, 1,325 people succumbed and by the epidemic's end, in 1645, it had touched the majority of families in the city.

The local manufacturers had better luck in 1698 when an Act was passed to make the River Aire navigable, giving a link to the Yorkshire coast and parts of the Continent for their products. Later, the Leeds and Liverpool canal opened up easier trade routes with West Lancashire.

The clothing trade, in particular, was boosted by the arrival of Jewish immigrants from Eastern Europe and Russia, and Leeds showed its ability to welcome and assimilate such immigrants; especially those with sought-after skills. Althoug some of the arrivals had difficulties initially, many of them prospered in later years and others rose to the very pinnacle of their calling and made a great contribution to the city's success.

Famous local 'names' over the years have included Sir William Sheafield, a noted classical scholar and founder of the Grammar School in 1552; Christopher Saxton, geographer to the first Queen Elizabeth; John Smeaton, builder of the Eddystone Lighthouse; and Matthew Murray who, although not born in Leeds, was an 'adopted son' with many inventions to his credit.

When World War One came a long there was to be no standing back and concentrating on commerce and the name of the locally raised regiment of volunteers, the 'Leeds Pals', was well known on the Western Front, whenre it suffered heavy casualities in the Battle of the Somme, in July 1916. The 'Pals' were highly regarded as matching up to the best standards of the regular army. Those who survived came back to the city whose diverse industries had prospered and, in the next two decades, the gaps between the villages which had surrounded Leeds were subject to all manner of development, especially of 'back-to-back' terraces, until the more open layouts of council estates began to eat into the surrounding countryside.

The slogan 'Leeds Leads' was no idle boast and the excellence of the city's central shopping area attracted customers from far and wide. Like so many things that had become an accepted way of life, that process was to continue until the advent of television and supermarket shopping would bring the benefits on those whose judgement the jury is still out.

Since that map was drawn, the town had grown to the point where it could be regarded as a city when an artist penned this panoramic view from an early railway bridge crossing the River Aire. In doing so, he marked the start of a 'Leeds Look' which developed consistently over 150 years and some of it is still recognisable today.

From *The Illustrated London News Social History in Victorian Britain*, by Christopher Hibbet (published by Angus & Robinson), it depicts the early days of the railways which transformed Victorian Britain and thrust Leeds into prominence in a transport system which would dominate travel to and from the city almost until the arrival of the M1 and M62 motorways.

Ironically, those same motorways helped mark the beginning of the end for thousands of miles of what was, arguably, the finest railway system in the world. The infamous 'Beeching cuts' on Britain's rail system certainly destroyed, in the Leeds area, a network of suburban lines that, if left, by the time of writing could have developed into one of the finest city rail systems in the country.

All the railway property and equipment in this view has long gone, with the exception of two items – one of the two stone towers which appears near the centre of the engraving, and the bridge in the foreground from where the drawing was made.

Both were retained with a view to preservation and/or refurbishment, but it has not quite worked out like that; the once-fine balustrades on the bridge have, in particular, suffered badly from vandalism. The long wall (left, centre) marked the boundary between Bean Ing Mills (now the site of the Yorkshire Post Newspaper Building), and a railway goods yard.

The railway lines on the right ran down from the bridge to the Central Station, in the distance, with the Great Northern Hotel (later the Wellesley), standing prominently near the right-hand side of the picture.

All those lines and the station buildings were carried on viaducts or man-made embankments which were a tribute to the foresight, business acumen, blood and sweat of the railway planners and builders. There would probably have been tears, too, had they known that the whole lot would be torn down and removed before the end of the 1960s.

The Aireside Centre development and the Holiday Inn Crowne Plaza now stand on land returned to the level of the water meadows where cattle had grazed alongside the river before the arrival of Benjamin Gott to erect his wooden mill at Bean Ing, in 1792, thus helping topropel Yorkshire into the forefront of the textile industry.

The railway navvies had worked miracles in meeting the demands of the architects. Some of the stone work was so massive (as in Great Northern Street near the present Royal Mail building), that demolition work was long delayed and traces of the original bridge wall remain to this day.

Morning and evening rush-hour travellers, up-tight and road-rage conscious, mind find it impossible to imagine that the gear-grinding mass crawl of rubber and metal at the 'Kirkstall lights' criss-crosses the foreground of what was once this idyllic scene. Cattle were lowing and strollers taking the evening air, rooks floated idly around the tower of the abbey. *Kirkstall Abbey, Yorkshire*, by Thomas Girtin, is one of the Victoria and Albert's print room treasures and a sorry reminder of what we have lost.

Pavements ('causeways', locally) and a paved roadway indicate growing prosperity in this 1830s view of Briggate. Street lamps indicate a degree of sophistication and ladies, and the 'gentry', are in evidence.

About the same year, gracious living was also depicted in this drawing by N. Whittock, engraved by J. Rogers. It shows Harewood House (which might have been in the Home Counties so far as the majority of Leeds citizens were concerned), with deer in the park, a sailboat on the lake and a parasol-equipped lady guarding her complexion from even the meagre sunlight.

Meanwhile, downtown the centre of Leeds was almost light-years from the 24-hour city so earnestly desired by some of today's planners and politicos. Even the trams which started that line of progress, and for which it became famous, had not arrived on the scene when some unknown photographer patiently set up his apparatus in what was to become the City Square. A water cart, such as was used to keep down the eternal dust, stands outside Mill Hill Chapel and the Peel Statue stood guard before the old Post Office at the bottom of Park Row, with the old St Anne's Cathedral at the top.

The fine lines of the Leeds Markets Building, better known to most 'Loiners' simply as Kirkgate Market, are well worth a moment's reflection on what appears to have been a quiet Sunday around the turn of the century.

12

Kirkstall Abbey

Although Kirkstall Abbey had existed outside the town boundary for several hundred years before it could officially be regarded as a part of Leeds, few true citizens would fail to lay claim to this magnificent ruin which has become a major tourist attraction.

Built between 1152 and 1182, and a victim of the Dissolution in 1539, its influence spread throughout the surrounding area for its occupants were industrious, but not perhaps enough, and they did suffer hard times.

Nearly a century ago, it would have been a determined visitor who braved the journey to Kirkstall through the squalor of the city's western inner suburbs, smoke-grimed by local industry, streets packed with tight lines of back-to-back houses on the valley's slopes, and a road crammed with great horse-drawn wagons, countless drays, and edged by busy workshops, warehouses, furnaces and belching factory chimneys.

But for those who did – as with today's visitors – there would be mixed feelings at what they found. When the ruins stood on open ground, and were covered in ivy in many parts, they were oft-sketched and painted, as per the undated picture printed here.

Kirkstall Abbey became an attraction to passing train passengers and was certainly one of the more picturesque structures to be seen on a train journey through the West Riding, but decisions to strip away its ivy sometimes left it looking cold and gaunt and detracted from its beauty.

That is a matter of opinion, but, of course, not being able to enjoy the rural settings of Rievaulx or Fountains, Kirkstall faces the fact that its once idyllic setting is now anything but that; nevertheless, it is regarded with great pride by local people who are fiercely protective of their locality's 'independence' – whatever the rest of the citizens of Leeds might feel about 'Kirkstall belonging to the city!'

For the record: In December 1888 the Trustees of the Earl of Cardigan offered Kirkstall Abbey and the nearby Abbey House for sale by auction, but the property failed to reach the reserve price of £10,000. At this point, Col. John North, who had made a cast fortune in South America, purchased the Abbey for presentation to the people of Leeds.

Among the many people who sketched the abbey was 'Thack', a long-time *Yorkshire Evening Post* cartoonist, whose nightly offerings were supplemented by occasional series on castles, countryside, market towns and points of interest. His drawing of the abbey was printed on 19 July 1968.

An earlier, undated view of Kirkstall Abbey. This engraving reveals the stark outline of the ruins following the Dissolution; but the two swans on the left are a stark reminder that, for several hundred years, even worse things were to affect the River Aire as pollution turned it into a poisonous soup.

Across the road from the Abbey is Abbey House Museum, surrounded by gardens whose spring and summertime flower displays are legendary. Once the gatehouse of the abbey, it later became a farmhouse. Today its outstanding attractions are the reconstructed streets of Victorian and Edwardian shops, workshops and dwellings which are particularly popular with school parties. There is a large car park and the museum is well-served by various bus routes from the city-centre area.

DOWN BY THE RIVERSIDE

Historians, it has oft been said, can never agree on anything, and recent television programmes on history, topography, archaeology, architecture and various other subjects only serve to underline that the same could be said of specialists in many fields.

But research into the beginnings of Leeds has reached a fairly common agreement: that the city began where Leeds Bridge spans the River Aire, at the foot of Briggate, where what would become known as Sheepscar Beck joined the main stream.

There is a good deal of evidence that the town began to spread out from that point, and that in the 13th century Briggate, which most people recognise as the city's main street, ran northward from the bridge (and almost certainly took its name from it).

The original narrow stone bridge was an area chosen by local cloth merchants to display their wares, thus catching visiting customers early. The original structure was improved by various widening schemes, then replaced by the existing bridge in the late 19th century.

This engraving depicts the old Leeds Bridge about 1849, with Briggate climbing away into the distance – and some artist's licence in the placing of Trinity Church tower. Present-day soap powder salesmen would have a field day with such customers as the lady optimistically hanging out the washing to the left of the bridge.

Later, the Crown Point (1842), Victoria (1839) and Wellington bridges were added to aid traffic flow, with subsequent improvements and additions being made to all three structures.

Almost immediately downstream of the warehouses depicted in the first picture, barges equipped with sails and able to navigate to and from the east coast were able to use the wharves. Dominating the scene is a seven-storey warehouse built in the late 1820s to handle the ever-increasing transfer amd storage of goods.

Wherever there are workers, you can usually find watchers. Men busy at work on barges around the huge warehouse, by then equipped with two crane housings, are being watched by 'railing leaners' while tqo ladies stroll by. Much damage was done here by a big fire in the 1960s. Today, 'town houses', a hotel, restaurant and other enterprises have replaced most of the buildings pictured, or have been incorporated into sustantially renovated and refurbished structures.

A closer look at barges and 'wharfees' at work on a brighter day, with cranes busy all along the riverside and smoke from a barge's stove-pipe chimney indicating that dinner time might well be at hand. The clue to the advance in years since the last picture was taken lies in the crossbars of telephone poles apparently erected on the roofs of some of the warehouses.

Looking east towards the bridge, this picture reveals the emergence of a channel (behind the shed in the foreground) which marked the end of the race from King's Mill. At the time of writing, there was speculation that archaeologists, working in Sovereign Street car park, had found what were believed to be the remains of King's Mill.

Leeds Bridge made history in an entirely new way when, in 1888, French-born artist, Louis Le Prince, took this sequence – the world's first-ever moving pictures – of a horse-drawn wagon moving across the bridge.

THE TELEVISION TOWN HALL

Although he dreamt of and planned his fair share of imposing structures, Cuthbert Brodrick (pictured here) could not have seen in his wildest dreams a situation under which one of his creations would be seen by millions of people, sometimes night after night, and in full colour.

TV news editors, producers and others in the media have consistently used a 'backdrop' of a shot of Leeds Town Hall on hundreds of television news and specialised programmes to emphasise the 'municipal' nature of the item being shown.

'Pity is', commented a Leeds City Council member, 'it never says that it's our town hall. But at least people will recognise that is better than 'owt south of Watford!'

It was either tea break time (if there were such things in those days), or a Sunday when this photograph of the Town Hall was taken during its period of construction in 1858. Only one human appears, perhaps finishing off a bit of pointing, or tying his bootlace, at the foot of the steps. The fine lines of Cuthbert Brodrick's structure up to clock level are marred by the somewhat rickety scaffolding of the incomplete tower and dome. The famous lions had yet to arrive (in the late 1860s) and a skyward-pointing cart, smokeless tar boiler and scattered building blocks indicate that 'the lads' just dropped everythingand headed for the pub when the working day ended.

The full spleandour of Brodrick's creation can be seen in this picture taken some years after its completion. In later years the effect of the great spread of steps was spoiled, some felt, by the erection of a ramp from Oxford Place (on the left, leading up to the building, and just below where the stone lion stared curiously at the photographer) Queen Victoria's statue on the right, was later moved from this prime spot to a controversial site at the university end of Woodhouse Moor, in the area just to the right of what is now the Feast and Firkin public House.

Meanwhile, another statue removed from the city centre, this time from near the top of Albion Street, is now located across Woodhouse Lane from the Queen Victoria statue and near the old Almshouses on Raglan Road. It is that of Revd Samuel Marsden, born at Farsley in 1764, who went out to Australia to work as a missionary. However, he achieved national fame – and hence the statue – for bringing back a onsignment of prime Australian wool in 1807, thus helping to found the Yorkshire–Australian woollen industry links which broight enormous wealth, and thousands of jobs, to the county. He died in 1838.

At Farsley, there is a memorial garden to Revd Marsden. It was presented to the local authority for the benefit of the people of Farsley by the late A.W. Hainsworth, a well-known local mill owner, and the great-grandfather of Mr Richard Hainsworth who kindly supplied us with the 1832 map of Leeds in the introductory chapter.

The full impact of atmospheric pollution is striking in this September 1956 view of a totally black Town Hall. The much newer Brotherton Wing of Leeds General Infirmary (on the right) already showed streaks of grime on its walls and a pall of Leeds 'clag' is evident to the south. But there was still two-way traffic along Great George Street amd a fair selection of Rolls-Royce, Jaguar and Riley cars gives proof to the old saying: 'Where there's muck there's brass!' A good point, though: there is not a piece of litter to be seen!

The smoke, soot and general grime of the Leeds atmosphere soon wiped out the pristine appearance of the new town hall, and it had almost turned black by the time this picture was taken on a sunny winter's day around the turn of the century. A horse-drawn cab waits for business by the statue, but signs of transport progress are in the air: overhead there are tram wires and a loop of tracks is in the bottom left-hand corner. Meanwhile, the scaffolding surrounds one of the tower sections of Oxford Place Chapel. Over the years, views have been expressed that the visual appeal of several British cities would have been increased and traffic congestion reduced had they opened up more squares, especially at bust intersections: a sort of Parisienne 'let traffic sort itself out' attitude. Had that applied, this view shows that Leeds would have had a head start in what was best known as Victoria Square.

FAMOUS THOROUGHFARES

Unlike the medieval streets of York – the pride of the county – which in style could hardly be likened to any place abroad, the main streets of Leeds have, surprisingly though it might be to 'Loiners', often struck a chord in the minds of overseas visitors. In the hey-day of the inter-war years, during and post-World War Two, overseas visitors and returned Service personnel alike were wont to remark on these similarities.

During that period, Boar Lane, running from City Square to Briggate, had class: well-designed buildings and 'respectable' shops, substantial banks, offices and well-known restaurants looked out onto a seemingly endless string of trams and other traffic. Some thought it had 'a touch of Paris, or some place on the Continent'.

Surprisingly, it often seemed busier than it does even in today's gridlock conditions. Narrow side streets led into a fascinating hinterland and Albion Street, the most important of those streets, was given an impressive start by the massive respectability of the Leeds Co-operative Industrial Society's main store.

Sadly, from the 1970s, many of Boar Lane's shops and buildings were allowed to run down, others were closed and the area took on a neglected look. But developments in the oast few years have brought i back into the mainstream of city life.

Park Row, meanwhile, always looked as if it had come straight out of the City of London's financial district, heavy with banks and assorted insurance offices. More than one Canadian said it reminded them of Toronto, as did the City Square end of Wellington Street.

The Headrow, opened out in the 1920s and 1930s from little more than a lane in some parts, aimed to be the style-setter for the city. It was in a class of its own, but failed to wear it in the style of Boar Lane.

While great new blocks housing stores, a huge cinema and offices were erected on its cleared north side, the south side clung on to most of its older structures. The exception was Schofields huge department store: a name as friendly, warm and welcome as everyone's favourite aunt.

If Boar Lane was busy, The Headrow's widening was a warning of things to come, for by the time the Inner Ring Road had become a neccesity, The Headrow was fast becoming a short-cut for lorry drivers on coast-to-coast journeys. Restrictions on traffic eliminated ome of the problems but an often ignored 'buses-only' policy still gives a 'through route' feeling, especially for pedestrians trying to cross the road.

Vicar Lane has a mix of activity which, if it was in New York, would put it in the Lower East or West Sides. The buildings in the section between the County Arcade and Kirkgate have style, but Vicar Lane never seemed to have quite the same attraction as the three thoroughfares mentioned above. Perhaps it is slightly peripheral, with people more likely to walk across it, e.g. from bus station to city centre, or city centre to Kirkgate Market, rather than walk along its full length. However, traffic-containing measures might well lead to an improvement in that respect.

Most famous of the main thoroughfares is Briggate: smart, boisterous, booming, sometimes near-bursting with people (and at one time trams), it is a cornucopia of commercialism. It has welcomed the great retail names since the turn of the century; the great entertainers (at the Empire) and live film stars (at the Paramount, later the Odeon complex). It has sold clothing, footwear and just about anything else shoppers seek, to generations of 'Loiners' and further millions from all over the North. It has had a café society all of its own (especially for Canadian and US servicemen in World War Two) and launched countless homeward-bound revellers safely to the suburbs via trams and buses.

Here is how those great thoroughfares developed:

Briggate - top to bottom

It is hard to imagine that Lewis's great store now stands just about where the building to the left of the then Corn Exchange (with clock) was positioned when this photograph was taken in the 1800s. This Exchange was built between 1826 and 1829 at the top of Briggate (in the foreground) between the Upperhead and Lowerhead Rows. The clock, and the statue or Queen Anne in the niche abover the door, came from the city's Moot Hall. However, the 'new' Exchange had a comparatively short history, for another competition won by Cuthbert Brodrick led to the unusually shaped and much larger building (dating back to 1862) which now stands at the top of Call Lane.

With the Corn Exchange gone, the oppertunity came to develop Briggate northward, toward North Street. It became 'New Briggate', or 'Upper Briggate' to some, and eventually embraced the Grand Theatre with its intricate canopy, and the Grand Arcade with its imposing entrance (on the left). On the right, by the open-topped tram, a banner proclaims, 'Parker's Hotel and Dining Rooms'. As for the lamp-standard, which also supports the tram wires, its fine decorative ironwork would horrify today's cost-conscious councils.

The 1829 Corn Exchange was swept away to allow the building of this block (now the site of Lewis's). Traces of some of the structures on this picture remain for this is the junction of Upperhead Row (later The Headrow) on the left and New Briggate. The whole of the block in the centre was demolished to make way for Lewis's store. But beyond that, the gate leading to St John's Church remains, along with a few of the buildings.

This faded photograph of Briggate below the Upperhead and Lowerhead Rows also reveals an attitude that would have hands raised in horror in today's council planning departments. Enourmous permanent signs, with raised letters, proclaim the Cash Boot and Clothing Company's premises, on the left, and a 'Slaughtering Price' sale poster is no less commanding. 'Good class clothing almost given away' claims another poster. More discreet, an early illuminated sin behind the fish bowl gas lamp on the right says: 'City Varieties, Twice Nightly'. Woe betide any husband spotted going up that yard when he was supposed to be at choir practice.

As the 'Gay Nineties' came in, Briggate started to take on some of the hustle, bustle and razzle-dazzle that made it famous throughout the North. Hope Bros dominated the skyline with a robust claim to be 'outfitters to all parts of the world'. The central cab rank sported broughams and hansoms and, for lesser mortals, an open-topped horse tram eased its way down the road. In 1899 the Queen's Arcade had been driven through (under the clock) but would still be known to many for years to come as 'Foster's Arcade' – the name of a leading shop on the site.

Still on the west side of the street, this stretch of shops, which was opposite the then 'Shambles', was torn down in 1903 to allow Albion Place to be extended from Lands Lane into the main shopping street. Perhaps the message had got around because the two carts on the left are laden with rubble from a partly boarded-up shop; the café next door had a bill up saying it had moved to Commercial Street, and the Hygenic Gas Stove Co. had put up the shutters. Apparently not superstitious, a lady on the extreme right was standing under a ladder.

In the early 1990s 'boaters' were in for men. In fact, hardly anyone in the picture is without headgear of some sort – a message there for today's clothing trade! Huge signs were still in fashion, with 'Boots Cash Chemists' prominent on the right.

Looking a little like they might have been designed for a bus station in Milan, Cairo or Granada, rather than a wet and windy night in Leeds, these tram shelters were built on part of the old horse cab ranks in the centre of Briggate, just up the road from the old Imperial Hotel (the black building on the right). Not quite so dingy as they looked, the shelters were witness to countless 'goodnight sweetheart' kisses as young ladies were seen off to the suburbs after a night at 'the pictures'.

Forward to the 1930s...the traffic lights are at red on the Briggate–Commercial Street corner, with trams outnumbering cars four to two. The large, light-coloured building on the left was Hitchen's, now long gone but once one of the city's most famous stores. The front of the leading tram carries an advertisement for Melbourne Ales, brewed in the city; the one side promotes Yorkshire Relish, an equally popular product.

A drawing made from the Briggate–Boar Lane corner, and a flashback in time, this depicts an earlier age when the Albion Hotel and Lockhart's Cocoa Rooms (on the right) looked across the street at buildings where, today, fast food establishments hold sway. The Albion was built in 1824 and rebuilt in 1874, being finally demolished in 1928. As with a number of old drawings and engravings, there appears to be some doubt as to whether 'keep left' rules were being observed.

Briggate's great crossing, at its meeting with Lower Briggate, Duncan Street (to the right) and Boar Lane (left), in 1903. With no traffic lights to control them, horse-drawn and electric trams, barrow boys, bicyclists, midden carts (for outside lavatory emptying) and what-have-you were supervised by a traffic policeman while a tram bearing the name of a famous Leeds store clatters across before him. Meanwhile, 'jay-walkers', the vast numbers of which continued to stagger American visitors to Leeds as late as the 1980s, take their myriad courses across the road.

A view of the Holy Trinity Church, Boar Lane, in the mid-19th century is blocked now by taller structures. This stretch of the west side of Lower Briggate had not changed much in 200 years when

this photograph was taken. The old building with dormer windows was believed to be of 16th-century origins. Just lower down. Pickard's Wine & Spirit Merchants boasted bat-wing doors that would have done credit to a Western saloon, and the stone setts must hav shaken the very livers of horse bus passengers.

Few city clocks were better known, or the contents or ownership of the shop it marked than was the 'Tempus Fugit' timepiece of John Dyson & Sons; a business which had been founded in Lower Briggate in 1865. Its superb window displays of jewellery, clocks, watches and silverware were a magnet women shoppers could not resist, even if their male companions tried hard to do so.

While hansom cabs and broughams wait for custom in the centre of the street, an open-topped horse bus waits on the east side of Lower Briggate, ready for off on a journey to the industrial and thickly populated residential areas south of the River Aire.

Boar Lane - east to west

Can you believe it? This was the Briggate entrance to Boar Lane before it was widened in 1867. The Central Shawl and Mantle Warehouse is on the right, the Golden Star pub on the left. As ever, it seems, the tower of Holy Trinity church will not be missed out! It pokes above the roof on the right.

The layout and construction of the re-laid tramway crossing at the junction of Boar Lane and Briggate, in 1899, was a tribute to its designers and builders. Not only did it necessitate fairly tight curves, the falling gradient into Lower Briggate also added to the problems of the designers. In the final analysis, however, it was the navvies such as those seen here who had the job of fixtting and fixing the complex trackwork with, no doubt, plenty of evidence from the watching throng...

With the trackwork complete, trams were able to clatter merrily from Duncan Street to Boar Lane, although an absence of traffic lights in those earlier times seemingly required two policemen to control the flood of jay-walkers etc. The shape of things to come lies in the rather posh open-top car emerging from Lower Briggate to the right. Well-known shop names here include Saxone Shoes (immediate left) and Gallons (on the right at the top of Lower Briggate).

Travelling west, then looking back, we can see Doyle's Glass shop on the lefty, the White Horse Restaurant further along on the right and the Grand Café and Restaurant whose canopy is on the right. The famous York House premises of Dunn & Co., hat makers, is in the right foreground. Meanwhile a Headingly tram, with the driver on an open platform, advances toward yet another policeman. He has his beady eye on a new model drop-head car being admired by a young man in shorts.

Here's a close-up of Dunne's famous hat emporium on the south side of Boar Lane, its windows topped with leaded lights and an assortment of coats-of-arms. It was opened in 1913 and lasted until the Boar Lane developments of the past few years.

Somewhat less stylish but no less famous in its day, Norton's Oyster Shop, whose exact position in Boar Lane is not clear, would have brought delight to today's fly-posting fraternity. Posters rekated to Rosenthal's Opera at the Amphitheatre, Inchbold's Account Book Manufactory, lectures by various local worties and a big political meeting at the Town Hall (were they at it already…?).

A handy short-cut to the trains, New Station Street came off Boar Lane where the two chaps are chatting under a lamp post in the corner. This row of shops changed hands many times over the years but they always seemed to be well patronised; perhaps because several of them sold specialist items. The one on the left, with the cabin trunks on the pavement, specialised in Frech and German fancy goods and manufactored ivory and horn handles for walking sticks and umbrellas.

Competition among the city's newspapers was intense in 1900, with the *Leeds Mercury* plastering the building at the corner of Albion Street (left) and Boar Lane with its posters for the Weekly Supplement. Signs ranging from the availability of false teeth to property adorned the building across the road, while Yorkshire Relish had the largest sign in distant Duncan Street. Taylor's, whoever they were, had an elevated sign – New York-style – over buildings on the right, near today's Marriott Hotel, thus cometing with the tower of Holy Trinity Church.

The main bar of the Griffin was popular with journalists of the 1950s and a wide range of other customers, all of whom were kept in order by a small but sturdy barmaid. Afficionados of Hollywood epics featuring bar-room brawls would have had a shock had they tried to lift any of the tables in this establishment. Picture: collection of the late Mr C.B Bairstow.

Almost opposite the empty shops in the top picture on the opposite page, the Griffin Hotel looked busy in this July 1947 scene. It was (and still is) on one corner of Mill Hill and Boar Lane, with the now-gone Boots the Chemist on the other.

Our journey along Boar Lane comes to a near end at West Bar where, in this somewhat grainy picture, the inevitable 'bobby' was busy on the left, sorting out cabs from carts.

A clearer day, a clearer view and yes, there is another 'copper' chatting with the tram inspector by the railings, as the tram on the left readies itself to take the right-hand curve to West Park and the leafy uplands of Headingly. This was the No.1 route on which trams started out from Roundhay, travelled down through the city, then out again to the north-western suburbs. A favourite local drink – Mather's Black Beer – is advertised on the flank of the leading tram. The Wine Lodge, with its amphitheatre-like bar, mighty cinema-style organ, and a giant ex-RUC doorman whose overcoat was big enough to make a bell tent, is to the left. A Grecian-style figure atop the semi-fortress of the Midland Bank holds the hand of a child and points downward as if to say what progress has done to the world. And yes, Leeds tram technology was so far advanced that they had their own electric signals – as on the striped posts in the foreground. Close examination reveals not a scrap of litter in the entire area. Not bad for 'one of those dirty northern towns', as they might have said in Hertfordshire.

City Square

The first point of interest to be seen by a large percentage of visitors to Leeds – certainly if they arrive by train – is City Square. As this set of photographs shows, there are few areas of the city which have undergone so many changes and yet retained some of their earliest features. And in terms of British history, it was not long before our first picture was taken that much of this ground had been open land, leading up toward Woodhouse Moor in the north-west and Kirkstall Abbey to the west.

A very early picture of what was to become City Square. Wellington Street comes in from the left with the tall building of Newsome & West standing in front of land on which the Majestic Cinema and the present Post Office would eventually be built. The horse tram tracks leading off to the right appear to terminate at the bottom of Park Row, where stands the old General Post Office. Assuming the other streets leading off to the left were retained after the demolition of much of the property, the one immediately to the right of Newsome's would become Quebec Street and that to the right of the Coloured Cloth Hall of 1758 (the circular building in the centre) would be Infirmary Street.

Believed to have been taken in 1879, this photograph reveals that the demolition men have done their stuff and the shape of City Square as we know it is starting to emerge. Newsome's building has vanished (top right) and construction of the Square's centrepiece is underway. The approach to the old Wellington Street Station (opened in 1846) and its roof outlined is behind the job of the crane. Originally owned by the Leeds and Bradford Railway, within a few years it was taken over by the Midland Railway (who were once reputed to have a grandiose plan that would have put their main station in the area around East Parade and Infirmary Street, not far south of the Town Hall). The large soot-begrimed building beyond the bill-boarded area is the old Queens Hotel. And, obviously, the billboard salesmen had been quick to cash in on this golden oppertunity for prime advertising space.

A much later but clearer view of the old Queens Hotel shows that the ground had been cleared to the left and Bishopgate Street established. This areas was altered again when new Queens Hotel was built and New Station Street brought around by the station to exit via the 'rubber road' under the arch at the left of the present Queens (i.e. approximately behind the lamp post to the left of this picture). The traffic density in Leeds at the time can be gathered from the signpost, directing traffic to Harrogate, Selby, York and along Boar Lane.

The formal presentation of the statuary in City Square to the City of Leeds took place with considerable pomp and ceremony in 1903. Thousands gathered here, including a not-inconsiderable number of troops, which no doubt pleased the Black Prince in his 'Forward Men' pose. The Standard Life Assurance Building, in the centre background, was demolished in the 1960s to make way for the controversial Norwich Union Building, whose design was much criticised by some, and which was itself flattened in 1995 to make way for a futuristic-looking structure. Many citizens found it more distasteful than the tower block offices of the 1960s, especially the new Magistrates Courts building at the corner of Park Street and Westgate.

At first glance, this splendid picture reveals a scene that might well have been in Rome (observe the charabanc waiting for tourists, and Granelli's ice cream cart in the foreground). Or could it have been Paris with all that striking statuary? Or a touch Germanic, considering that heavy-looking building in the centre? The true 'Loiner' only needs to see the tram on the left, of course, to know it is good old City Square, with a steam wagon chugging out of Aire Street across the bows of one of those new-fangled Model 'T' Ford wagons. The year was 1926.

The city's War Memorial was erected in the Square in 1922. It was moved to the Garden of Rest in The Headrow in 1937 and the angel taken to Cottingley. The old Queens Hotel can be seen on the right.

The Square was looking somewhat drab in October 1936. Trams ran up and down Park Row and along Infirmary Street. But there was no 'gyratory' system for traffic which scuttled merrily in all directions and parked likewise. The grime-coated Mill Hill Chapel (opened 1848 on the site of a previous chapel) and the surrounding buildings look drab indeed.

Apart from the weather, there was a great lift in spirits and outlook for 'Loiners' when this striking display appeared in 1937 to mark the Coronation of King George VI and Queen Elizabeth (the late Queen Mother). The city's coat-of-arms owls were prominent on the structure. All the buildings to the right (in Infirmary Street) were subsequently demolished. An entrepeneurial Sammy Ledgard's single-deck bus is crossing the bows of three of Leeds City Transport's distinctive round-top double-deck jobs.

It did not take all that many years for the new Queens Hotel to lose its pristine appearance and start to take on the same grimy look as its predecessor. In the late 1960s the *Yorkshire Evening Post* launched a campaign for the more grubby Leeds buildings to be given a wash and brush-up, and a 'freshened up' Queens Hotel started to emerge from the dirt-covered façade that had resulted from falling soot and rising traffic pollution.

The Queens Hotel and adjacent buildings were still being completed when a photographer braved the city's regular smoke haze to get this aerial picture of City Square. Workmen were also hard at it re-aligning the tram tracks through the Square, and in Infirmary Street leading off to the right. This is one of the few aerial pictures which gives a clear impression of the size of the Post Office block in those days. Barges are tied up in the River Aire basin (top left), and the platform roofs of City Station are behind the Queens.

White bands painted on tram poles, lamp standards and pavement edges; cars with shrouded headlamps; Air Raid Shelters surrounding the Black Prince all mark this as wartime City Square (it was November 1943). There is a large static water tank in front of Mill Hill Chapel (foreground). Showing at the Majestic: Tyrone Power in *Crash Dive*.

A more recent (but already dated) picture of the Square. Most of the cars will have gone to the scrap heap, and what metal would be recovered from the Norwich Union Building, demolished in 1995.

This artist's impression shows the building that succeeded the old Noriwhc Union structure at the corner of City Square and Park Row. Compared with the first of our City Square pictures, the effects of a century of development are quite striking, to say the least.

Park Row

Arguably the most elegant street in the city centre – 'It should be, that's where t'brass is', a true Loiner might say – the entrance to Park Row is seen here in a distant view from Bishopgate Street. The old West Bar entrance to Boar Lane is to the right and, as the caption to this engraving says, 'the city had some comely architecture'. On the left is the porticoed entrance to the former Court House where the judges sat before the Town Hall was opened in 1858. In the centre, at what is now the corner of Boar Lane and City Square are the magnificent Commercial Buildings, opened in 1829. Amazingly, they were to last for only a little over 40 years, being replaced by a structure of far less taste and that, in turn, was eventually replaced by the box-like tower block which still stands here, but has been much less-maligned than the Norwich Union block on the north side of the Square which was demolished in 1995.

Subsequently, the Court House became the General Post Office and Peel's Statue, on the fringe of what would become City Square, is fading out of the picture on the left. Park Row runs off to the right. Surprisingly, the Post Office building was demolished in 1901.

A little further up Park Row, this shot was made at the Bond Street crossing, with the City Museum building on the left. The old St Anne's Cathedral is in the distance, where The Headrow now slices across Park Row. In 1901, the cathedral was bought for £46,000 by Leeds Corporation for road-widening purposes. It was replaced in 1904 by the present cathedral, standing further up Cookridge Street.

Taken at almost the same spot nearly half a century later, this picture reveals a device that made history: traffic lights on this crossing were believed to be the first of their kind in the country. Note that partly through the Luftwaffe bombs in World War Two, the front of the Museum had been removed. Changes since this picture was taken include the Midland Bank building erected on the former museum site. The first building on the right was demolished and replaced by a new Westminster Bank.

It was the grime as much as the architecture that immediately distinguished the difference between old and new buildings in the first half of the 20th century: witness this view of the bottom end of Park Row. 'City gents' on the left, naturally complete with rolled umbrellas, match the elegance of what, no doubt, radiated from the ladies' fashions in the still much-missed windows of Marshall & Snelgrove on a site now occupied by Lloyd's Bank.

The Headrow - east to west

The Lowerhead Row had been widened to near today's width when this picture was taken, probably in the late 1930s. Phillips Stores already carried a sign reading 'The Headrow'. The owners of the shop had corrupted a famous Guiness slogan (although not from the one on their gable end) on a poster in their window reading: 'Any one of our lines is good for you, but think what TOUCAN do.' The furniture shop of Waldenburg Bros (established 1896) and Allpass & Co were prominent on the right where a parked D.C.L. United Yeast Co.'s van was no doubt delivering to H. Brown & Sons, grocers and bakers.

The archway on the right was the entrance to Rockley Hall Yard, originally the site of Rockley Hall, the home of John Harrison, a great Leeds benefactor in the 17th century. He founded St John's Church, near the top of Briggate. Married in 1603, he lived at Rockley, then an old Tudor mansion of mainly timber construction. Portions of it remained until the early part of this century.

To the left, on Vicar Lane, Henry Wigfall's cycle shop looked clean and sprightly, with the Nag's Head pub next door but one ('concert room and light refreshments') while Hartley's Music Stores, on the extreme left, were pushing the sales of His Master's Voice records.

The mind boggles at the time and energy needed to set-up this display every morning, then remove it every night at the shop of A. Lewis, General Manufacturers, of 17 Lowerhead Row. The picture was taken in the 1920s when they sold sports and fancy goods, musical instruments, tools and...maybe even a kitchen sink!

Moving up the Lowerhead Row in 1928, we come to the Briggate crossing with Upperhead Row beyond. New Briggate is off to the right, being surveyed by the traffic policeman. The area has been transformed with bunting and flags for Civic Week, the Aussie flag on the left no doubt raised hopes – or anguish – for Headingly matches to come and others already gone...Burton's were to retain the shop on the left-hand corner for years to come and the Horse and Trumpet pub, on the left up the street, is still there. A small Schofield's Chocolates sign topped the shop doorway on the right, but the *Evening Post* was in prime position with its large illuminated sign.

The same location on what must surely have been a Sunday in the late 1920s. The Town Hall's dome can just be seen in the distance but soon everything on the right of Upperhead Row, which was to be doubled in width, would be swept away. The Paramount Picture house, later the Odeon, would be erected on the immediate right and Lewis's mighty store would rise where Mr Skelton, hosier and shirt maker, had his shop next door to Schofield's corner chocolate shop.

Here is the proof: it is 27 March 1932. The Paramount has been built and is showing Francis A. Mangan's *Creation in Blue*, with the mighty Wurlitzer organ entertaining during the intervals. The 'bobby' on traffic duty was having an easy time of it and his position marks the width of the old Upperhead Row where Schofield's shop had been. The steel work on the front of Lewis's shows the new width of what would soon be renamed The Headrow.

The finished job (before extensions) and an indicator on the upper wall of Lewis's corner shows that £171,347 had 'to date' (unknown) been raised for Leeds Infirmary. This angle clearly shows why such massive evacuations were needed for the store, especially at the west (Town Hall) end. Floors well below the ground level at that end were at ground level by the time they had reached New Briggate (on the right foreground). Shoppers in the new basement were astonished to learn that there was still a 'works' department below them!

Now a look back in time and direction. It is 1929 and preparations for widening the Upperhead Row had commenced (on the near left and at the New Briggate corner beyond). The Horse and Trumpet sign is on the right, just beyond what is believed to be one of the famous 'bull-nose' Morris cars which would probably bring a fortune if offered for sale today. And how about the stylish WU 2596 coupé on the left! Did it belong to dome reader's great-grandfather?

A last look back at Upperhead Row before it split into Woodhouse Lane (leading off to the left) and Guildofrd Street, from where the picture was taken. The Victoria Arcade (site of Schofield's) is on the right with Lands Lane just beyond. On the immediate right, with the massive lamps, is the well-ornamented Cock and Bottle free house which sold Bass on draught and, of course, Tetley's. One thing is clear, it must have been a Sunday, the gates are closed on Victoria Arcade and the blinds are down in most shops.

The caption on this old print places 'Ye Olde Kings Arms' in Upperhead Row, but the author has been unable to pin-point its location. Judging by the sunlight, it must have been on the north side. Nor can we give the date, although the decorations and the words 'Long May She Reign' surely show the period as Victorian. And there appears to be a portrait of the Queen in the central upper window. Nor do we know if the chap on the roof was the landlord, Mr Pickersgill, no doubt pleased with his efforts – and rightly so.

The corner of the building on the extreme left, and the arch of the distant arcade entrance to the right, are the clues which mark this 1920s view as the site of what would be one of the biggest transformations in the city up to that time. It would not be long before the row of shops in the centre, which were at the bottom of Woodhouse Lane where it joined the then Upperhead Row, was demolished to make way for the huge excavation in which Lewis's mighty new store would be built. Mark Lane which, strangely enough, seemed wider then than it does today, runs off to the left. The archway on the right was that of the Victoria Arcade, on Schofield's site.

The shops in the previous pciture had stood where the west end of Lewis's excavation ate into the bottom of Woodhouse Lane. Upperhead Row was being opened up to the left. There is little or nothing left today of any of the buildings across Woodhouse Lane, apart from the tower of St Anne's cathedral on the right.

Now we are looking west in the same area on a much later date. The gates have gone from the Victoria Arcade on the left. Schofield's store has a new frontage and is spreading towards Albion Street, no doubt to consternation of the regulars at the Cock and Bottle. The good news is that a London Midland & Scottish Railway horse-drawn dray is delivering beer to the pub and...could that rather splendid Woseley car be the one in which *Yorkshire Evening Post* journalists and photographers were sometimes taken to posh assignments by a staff driver? Can you believe, they were sometimes mistaken for gentlemen of the constabulary?

Our best efforts failed to pull up the name of this inn at Guildford Street. Did it stand on the site of the present Guilford Hotel? Or did it give its name to Green Dragon Yard, which still exists? Whatever the case, the pub was certainly long gone by the time of our next and final picture of The Headrow, which was taken in the early 1930s.

And here we are at the end of our Headrow journey. With Park Row branching off to the right, we are looking east with the former (and much missed) headquarters of the Leeds Permanent Building Society on the left. The matching frontages of the buildings, which still exist, were being completed up toward the Albion Street crossing. Many years later, Headrow House would be built on the site of the remaining old building beyond the lorry at the top of the gradient.

Vicar Lane

Although the owners of business premises, and particularly shops in Vicar Lane would no doubt argue the point, general opinion seems to be that this thoroughfare does not have the charisma or flair of Briggate or The Headrow. Perhaps the impression arose because it has long been a street which most people crossed rather than walking along its length.

One mystery persists: most 'Loiners' believe that Vicar Lane runs clean from the Inner Ring in the north to the Corn Exchange in the south. Some maps show that its southern end used to terminate at Lowerhead Row and Market Street completed the section between there and Kirkgate. The rest was New Market Street – it all depends on whose map you take as being correct! Most would stick to Vicar Lane.

However, here we are at the Kirgate junction around 1930 with a traffic policeman on duty. McQuat's Bar is on the left and the nearby street signs clearly show Kirkgate and Vicar Lane.

This much earlier picture, in the 1880s, shows the arch leading to Wood Street, which no longer figures on the maps of the central area, but this was roughly in line with the County Arcade. Mr White, at No 17 (first shop on the right of the arch), offered teeth extraction. Sam'l Saipes (No.19) boasted 'The greatest house for tailors and dressmakers trimmings'. And through the archway itself was the Boot and Shoe inn.

'Tram wires' slice across the skyline where the imposing market buildings tower on the corner of Kirkgate and Vicar Lane (or was it Market Street?).

It would be the rush hour in the 1923 view of the Lane with the heavier traffic heading away from the city centre. There is a line of trams with the No.244 heading for Meanwood (they had destination boards at the back as well as the front in those days). McQuat's 'First Class Bar' is on the left. Picture courtesy of Mr M.J. Collinson, of Ebor Gardens Estate, Leeds.

Streets, Lanes, Snickets and Ginnels

Taken in the late 19th century, this remarkably clear picture of Albion Street has Albion Place running off on the right with a famous old shop sign on the corner. Both streets were well and truly cobbled. It must have been a warm day: solicitor J.H. Milner, on the top floor on the right, has his windows open; and the Leeds and Pudsey Liberal Unionist Association, and the Yorkshire Liberal Unionist Federation had their blinds lowered on the first floor. In the late 1960s Yorkshire Post Newspapers Promotions and Publicity Department occupied the first florr of the building on the left. The archway beyond it led to the 'reel store' where reels of paper were kept for the printing of the *Yorkshire Post* and *Yorkshire Evening Post*. Imagine the effect the huge delivery trucks had on Albion Street traffic. Just one of the reasons the *YPN* moved to Wellington Street!

Another late-19th-century view, lower down the street, shows a horse bus crossing from Commercial Street to Bond Street, with the imposing Leeds and Yorkshire Assurance Co.'s building of 1855 in the background.

The city's business leaders were not slow in coming forward when it came to demonstrating civic pride. The Old Leeds Stock Exchange, in Albion Place, would have been welcome in many European cities where the residents thought themselves a cut above the English entrepeneurs elevated by the Industrial Revolution.

Come VE Day to mark the end of World War Two and the Leeds Co-operative Industrial Society did Albion Street proud with this display of flags and bunting at the lower end. The long-gone canopies were a welcome shelter for shoppers, as was the Co-op Café in the building on the right. A concert hall in the same building was the venue for many shows put on by local amateurs.

Not the best of days for shopping – Lands Lane today is rarely as quiet as in this non-pedestrianised view, with the homely old King Charles pub sandwiched between the bottom of the Victoria (Schofields) Arcade and the Theatre Royal, whose massive tower-borne water tank looked big enough to create a tidal wave from there to Boar Lane, should its fire-fighting system have ever been brought into action.

It is a sunny day and Commercial Street is thronged with shoppers. A young blade in a 'boater' turns to admire a very posh vehicle – probably a 'Roller' – registered U461. The building in the centre, at the corner of Commercial Street amd Lands Lane, was the site of the popular Betty's Café for many years.

Nearer the Briggate end of Commercial Street, this picture may have been taken before Betty's moved into the building on the immediate left, because a 'TO LET' sign appears in the first-floor window. Wray's Restaurant was on the right, as was (downstairs) The Mitre Pub which served excellent lunches and was popular with journalists, especially those on farewell parties from the nearby *Yorkshire Evening News* in Trinity Street.

Two new buildings in succession have replaced the one on the left since World War Two era picture was taken of East Parade. A traffic policeman directs a solitary cyclist across the empty void. Two lines of studs behind the 'bobby' indicate what must have been one of the longest 'Belisha Crossings' (later 'Zebra' crossings, now 'pedestrian' crossings), in the city. The central lamp standard bears signs with directions to Air Raid Shelters and the 'Public Gas Cleansing Centre', which probably caused 'Loiners' to say nasty things about the awful Hun. Unchained, un-cabled, untouched...a cycle leans against a pavement edge. On the left, a suitcase-carrying young soldier, apparently with family members in tow, is probably on his way to the Central Station.

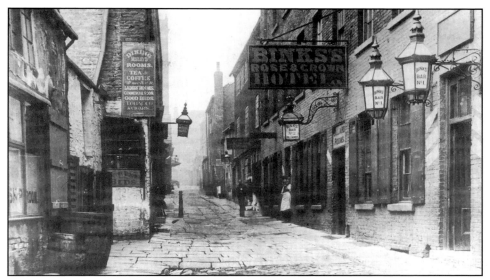

Not exactly the atmosphere for the sort of pavement café yearned for by some of the current crop of 'Let's make Leeds a 24-hour city' planners, the Rose and Crown Yard, off Briggate, is now the Queen's Arcade. However, it did offer a fair selection of facilities for its day: Marley's Dining Rooms, on the left, had tea and coffee rooms, ladies rooms, a commercial room and 'Good Beds for Travellers'. If that was not enough for overnight lodgers, Binks' No.1 and No.2 bars accross the setts and flags offered good ale and a billiards room.

What the Dickens...'Fish Street and The Shambles' says the caption. Fish street it might have been – Shambles it certainly was, with the offerings of local butchers displayed in conditions that were light years away from the freezer sections of today's supermarkets. For the benefit of 'incomers' Fish Street was little more than a 'ginnel' which ran between the top part of Kirkgate and Vicar Lane, with a 'snicket' running off to King Edward Street.

Famous far and wide, some of the great arcades of the city replaced squalid, dangerous streets and alleys in an area which had suffered from a shambles of appalling, crowded slums and workshops, with indescribable conditions so far as sanitation was concerned. Many of the changes that would banish some of those horrors came towards the end of the 19th century with splendid plans by the Leeds Estates Company to build an imposing set of office blocks and shops, of which the city could be proud.

Shown here (top) is the Briggate frontage with (left to right) the County Arcade, New Bond Street and Cheapside blocks, separated by Queen Victoria Street (left) and King Edward Street (right).

The central block contained the 'Empire Palace', or Leeds Empire, as it became generally known. The lower elevation shows the other end of the blocks in Vicar Lane. There is an office/shop section on the left; then King Edward Street; detail of the proposed and quite striking Dolphin Hotel block; Queen Victoria Street and, finally, the County Arcade block.

Even todat, what is left of these structures is a striking reminder of the city's proude past and the progressive entrepeneurs which it spawned.

The Arcades

Most of the discreet ladies and gents' items of clothing in the Cashdisia stores' windows on the left were rounded off in 11-pence 'steps' (rather like the 49p and 99p 'steps' in today's shops) in this 1900s picture. Forty years later, the Mecca Locarno dance hall – and its then young manager Jimmy Saville, with a tartan-dyed hairstyle – would become a magnate for 'jitterbug' fans long before he reached the heights of being knighted. Today, the County Arcade adds its charm to the acclaimed Victoria Quarter.

The efforts of an unknown contemporary artist reveal that long before city council planners had thought of a '24-hour Continental-style' atmosphere for Leeds, there was some quite considerable Continental style in the Queen's Arcade. The Industrial Revolution had produced the wherewithal for great iron roof spans and wrought-iron balcony railings, while finely decorated gas lamps gave a warm glow to enhance an atmosphere that many a European might well have envied. Today, European tourists still come to admire its charms.

The Victoria (or Schofields Arcade) is guarded by a grand set of gates during its Sunday closing. The 'L' shaped arcade led customers either into the store or, in inclement weather, it could be used as a dry route to Lands Lane (on the left). In due course the great arch and everything else in this block was demolished, to make way for Schofields huge new store (see the Great Stores section).

THE GREAT STORES

Ever since the town started to push northwards from Leeds Bridge its shops have been a magnet for visitors; first from nearby villages, then more distant towns, then even from other cities across the North. Originally they came in horse-drawn wagons and carriages, later by specially chartered buses and trains. Now they come by ferry and luxury coach from Germany, Holland and Belgium; and even by plane from Dublin, Belfast, Glasgow and Schiphol.

There are not, now, many of 'the great stores' of which Leeds was once so proud. In common with other great cities of the world, and particularly in the West, the advent of the shopping mall and out-of-own retail parks, discount centres and huge supermarkets has tempted people away from the great downtown stores where car parking is difficult, or even impossible, and (certainly in Britain) public transport is not all it used to be.

Not that every out-of-town retail outlet is all it is cracked up to be: buildings which, in many cases, are little more aesthetic than glorified aircraft hangars, often lack the comforts and style of the great stores. Admittedly, most of the shopping malls do better although the author well remembers that the effects of the stark Canadian winters had more to do with the provision of the enormous, undercover, front-runner Edmonton out-of-town complex in Alberta than did a desire to tempt people away from the log cabin Hudson's Bay-style stores of yesteryear.

Between the wars Leeds had, in many respects, such a complex in the area bounded by Vicar Lane, Boar Lane, Park Rowand the Headrow. Shoppers could enjoy a whole day in its great stores or, some would say, even in just one of them. They still cite good service, comfort, style, lots of facilities, restaurants, cafés, 'always something going on', even simply 'somewhere to sit down' as reasons for their popularity. Good enough reasons for signs that they may be making a come back.

Schofields had been established in the Upperhead Row for many years when this picture was taken at the entrance to the Victoria Arcade – 'Schofields Arcade' to many shoppers.

The company was in its 21st year at the time of this picture, showing a window display in the arcade.

'Profit by the square foot' merchandising was still a long way off when this 1926 study of Schofields millinery department revealed plenty of space for decorative palm trees and, literally, a wall of mirrors in whieh 'modem' could check-out the look of her latest likely purchase.

Many *Yorkshire Evening Post* readers wrote in to say that they had wept when the news broke that Shofields was to disappear. Asked to send in memories of the prestigious family store, customers and members of staff deluged the Editor with happy tales...Schofields had a reputation as a family store, and this picture shows a typical staff day outing before World War One. Mrs Ada Thurlow, of Laith Walk, Ireland Wood, Leeds, who submitted the picture to the paper, is the seventh from the left in the second row back. She wrote: 'The man ninth from the left in the same row (with bow tie) is Mr Snowden Schofield. The lady on his right became his wife.

By 1962 the rebuilding of Schofields store between Lands Lane and Albion Street was complete. The impressive Headrow frontage included a heated arcade at street level – a popular meeting place on chilly days.

Across the road, on the north side of the Headrow as it had then become, this huge excavation, reminiscent of a dry dock, appeared in the early 1930s. New Briggate was at the far end. Just how much of Lewis's great store is below ground level only becomes apparent in such pictures, which show work underway in July 1931. The cranes on the far skyline reveal where the new Paramount picture house was being built on the opposite side of New Briggate. (Photograph: Courtesy Lewis's)

The amount of shale in the strata around The Headrow and Albion Street brought problems for the builders of Lewis's and other large structures in the area. Here can be seen the massive amount of supports needed to contain the sides of the excavation, particularly on the north (Mark Lane) side where the tower of St John's Church overlooks the scene. Some idea of the depth of the foundations can be gained from the fact that the store's 'work's department' (left foreground) is nearly four floors below ground level at the top (Dortmund Square) end of the building. (Photograph: Courtesy Lewis's)

The left-hand corner entrance to Lewis's in this picture marks the point from where the two previous photographs were taken. Here is Lewis's in 1932, shortly after the store's opening, with crowds thronging The Headrow to see the giant shop; also the new Paramount cinema (just beyond the flags). (Photograph: Courtesy Lewis's)

Internally, Marshall & Snelgrove's was undoubtedly a store of great taste and style, and very popular with up-market shoppers. Its top two storeys an addition which caused some angst among the city's architects and Victorian building fans, was less stylish. But to step into this store from Bond Street was to leave everyday Leeds behind and, certainly in the mind's eye, enter the fashion salons of Paris. No wonder the female fashion writers of the city's newspapers favoured coffee in its excellent restaurant. Even if it was then back to Headingley on the tram for a fish 'n chip tea at Brett's...Curiously enough, that great stores atmosphere of latter-day Leeds can still be found, even today. But you have to be 12,000 miles away in David Jones's store in Sydney, Australia, to experience it!

TRANSPORT IN LEEDS

Since the author first came to Leeds – and probably long before that – there have been arguments about the best transport policy for the city. Wags and cynics alike might well ask: 'What policy?' And now that the interests of local government, national government, entrepreneurs, privatisation groups, environmental groups and other bodies are all involved with this question, there would sometimes seem to be no more hope of a clear solution than there has ever been.

It is arguable that several benefits of foresight were ruined by 'progress' – the killing-off of a first-class tramway system, much of it contained on dedicated tracks, is perhaps the most glaring example.

For years, Leeds had one of the bcst tramway systems in Britain, possibly the world. Trams usually got through whcn there was snow, fog and ice. They were particularly warm and friendly in winter and at all times seemed to knit the city together to create a metropolitan atmosphere which many felt was lost with their passing. Environmentally friendly, they were clean and reliable. And anyone who says they were slow has not driven in current rush hours in the city.

But a 'rush to the bus', plus political and financial arguments led to what many regarded as undue haste in their removal, especially outside the inner-city areas. As one enthusiast said, 'Apart from anything else, over the last quarter of a century, countless thousands would have been able to get to and from work on snowy days, instead of being cut-off in the suburbs.'

Likewise, Leeds might well have had one of the finest suburban railway systems in the country had not the Beching axe and similar problems to those affecting thc trams fallen upon thc extensive network of lines that criss-crossed and surrounded thc city. Ironically, a near-photocopy system in Maryland, USA, was retained and is efficient, progressive, profitable, and continues to bc extcnded.

Thankfully, a more commonsense approach has prevailed at what is now the Leeds Bradford International Airport. Long-term planning and steady growth has been accelerated in recent years. Considerable investment in new terminal facilities, runway lighting, car parking, and instrument landing systems have all helped to lift the airport into the international league table of services and, equally important, the airport's position on the British map gave it a good start in establishing increasingly popular 'hub and spoke domestic and near-Continent feeder services.'

Trams for Everyone

It was 'Hold tight,' from the conductor and 'Gee up,' from the driver when the horse trams ran up York Road. The box on the front of the tram was probably a 'mobile post box', as carried on many such vehicles years ago.

The steeper gradients of the Chapeltown service called for three horses to manage the double-deck, open-top trams, one of which is seen at the old Queen's Arms stop. It took three men to handle this rig – a far cry from today's one-man super buses carrying well over twice the load of the old timer.

Batty's 'Nabob' Pickles seem to have added their own piquancy to the days when this tram ran along Cardigan Road. The photograph was contributed by Miss G. Knowles, of Moortown, who explained that the tram was at the Cardigan Road terminus and the conductor (left) was Mr John Knowles, who lived in Burley and worked from the Headingley Tram Depot.

There were nearly enough uniformed crew members to start making a film about the American Civil War on this 'Tam O'Shanter' tobacco tram, decorated to some tune on the Cardigan Road route. Note the 'old masters' lamp illuminating the front destination board. There is a picture of an unidentified 'Royal' above the board, and another in the lower saloon window, but the exact nature or date of the event is unknown.

A far cry from push-button ticket and change machines and open-necked shirts: these smartly turned-out Leeds City Transport employees turned-up on the first electric tram to Rodley. Behind the tram and to the right was the Three Horseshoes pub, later renamed as the popular Rodley Barge.

There is a cheeky wind blowing and passengers are holding on to their hats and skirts as car No.133, proudly carrying a poster for the *Yorkshire Post*, sits in the late-afternoon sunshine outside the Corn Exchange. Magnification indicates that, yes, the driver does have an old sock on the hrake handle. As for that lamp at the top of the front stairs, no doubt Saturday Night revellers up there would bait the driver with a few verses of *Lead Kindly Light...*

Today the scene of nose-to-tail traffic for most of the day, the A65 at Guiscley sported wide open spaces on this day around 1910 when the tram terminus from Leeds was at the junction of Oxford Road. It was later extended to Harry Ramsden's at White Cross. Not a lollipop lady in sight in those hlissful days!

Looking like an early version of a Russian rocket launcher, the forward part of this contraption is the powered part of a steam tram with the passenger-carrying double-deck trailer behind. Several of these 'belching monsters' were in use between the steady demise of the horse trams and the arrival of electric cars. No.28, complete with 'cow-catcher' is at the New Inn terminus in Tong Road, where the crew took a breather (the driver probably needed one). What the top-deck passengers of the trailer experienced when windows needed to be opened on summer days is not recorded. Note that milk was being delivered direct from the churn in the trap on the left.

Here is another version of the steam tram near Shaw Lane, Headingly, on 10 May 1888. The home of Vctorian photographer Godfrey Bingley was nearby, and this excellent print was unearthed from a large collection of his pictures at Leeds University.

At most times of day you can expect to see between 50 and 100-plus vehicles on this stretch of Otley Road at its junction with Shaw Lane. But the tram conductor seems to be looking over the edge of the top deck to see where everyone has gone as No.4I ambles along, with what will become its rear indicator already changed for the return trip Chapeltown. The shops on the left, incidentally, have not changed much since this early 1900s shot, other than in terms of ownership.

Lonesome road: a Swinegate-bound tram has just left Middleton Woods, heading across country towards Parkside in the early 1950s. The foresight of the city fathers who advocated 'reserve tracks' for the city's tramway system was tragically spoiled by those who thoght that diesel buses were the answer.

No.602, pictured here between two of her older sisters in City Square, was one of the new streamlined rail cars (a 'supertram' in today's parlance), which had put places like Leeds and Blackpool well ahead of the field just at the time when the great brains of British transport planning started the great rush for the bus.

Just what an effect the change of buses had on the superb Leeds tramway system can be judged from the fact that this dedicated new tramway depot, opened at Otley Road, Headingley, in 1935, had been converted into a bus depot within a quarter of a century.

This 10-seater horse bus of Leeds City Transport trundled out to Old Farnley in 1906. A piece of cord which ran along the ceiling was connected with a bell beside the driver, who almost certainly also acted as conductor in view of the restricted space.

One of the big ex-London trams of the type on which the author had made hundreds of journeys around south London before many of them were transferred to Leeds. He was happy to renew his acquaintance, especially on cold winter's mornings. The last tram to run through City Square on 21 July 1956, No.542 was working the No.15 Whingate route and was cheered all the way. 'Tram nute' from all over the North were out and about that night, and as Mrs Gilbert Towers drove No.542 through City Square for the last time a trumpeter on board sounded the *Last Post*. It was not the *very last* tram to run in Leeds, a few were kept running until 1959 before the mighty enterprise which had grown from a horse-drawn service in 1871 was finally closed down. And Leeds was never to be quite the same again, for those metal tracks formed a network which residents felt held the city's suburbs together. The buses never created the same atmosphere.

Buses Galore

A three-in-hand horse bus, its driver well-wrapped against the weather, was ready for the 'off' when pictured outside an unidentified Leeds pub in 1900.

Private enterprise led to a fair amount of jockeying for position among horse bus drivers as they plied for passengers. This three-in-hand-powered job of Messrs Gills was outside the Bay Horse Hotel, Briggate, having loaded up for Hunslett Carr. Class distinction was evident, with only two smartly dressed passengers inside and 'everybody for thersen' on top. As for the advertisement – many of us thought 'Compo' was a cold cure. Perhaps memory plays tricks. Here it says 'washing for everything'.

This fearsome-looking contraption was an experimental chain-drive trackless car, or trolley bus, with the somewhat apprehensive driver and passengers ready for take-off. The 'king-size' mudguards and skirts were, presumably, to guard passengers and pedestrians from the whirling chains. The

picture is courtesy of Mrs Doreen Goodyear, of Horsforth, from the collection of her father, the late Mr Ernest Frank, who worked for Leeds City Transport from 1916 to 1960.

Also from Mr Frank's collection is this picture of a smart-looking conductor in the type of uniform worn around 1905.

On 20 June 1911, the Lord Mayor of Leeds, Wm Middlebrook, MP, opened the first British 'trackless car system'. Here No. 503, which made that first run, was brought to a halt several times by cheering crowds on the way to Farnley. Picture from Mr Peter Johnson.

What a magnificent monster! Chances are that the 'chara' body was taken off and replaced by a flat-bed lorry device during the week. But all of that was no concern to these ladies setting out in U-6001 from North Hill Tavern, Kirkstall Road, for a bone-shaking, teeth-rattling, hat-wobbling, solid-tyred day out.

Now we are getting somewhere...all polished-up and the 'works' covered in. An attractive group of lasses all ready for a trip in the first coach owned by Wallace Arnold. It was this type of charabanc in which Mrs Elsie Pullans (who supplied the picture) made her first trip – to Torquay – in 1926.

All set for Dewsbury Road and Middleton as a lady passenger smiles at the pose set by the conductor – his boots as shiny as his bus in the early days of private competition.

The Corporation experimented with a variety of buses over the years. This Halley model of 1928 was a six-wheeler with a businesslike look. Picture courtesy of Mr Peter Johnson.

If it is not too near a pun, the name of Sammy Ledgard was legendary. He was one of the earliest, and certainly the most persistent, private bus operators in the Leeds area and here is one of his 'charas' outside the Nelson Hotel, Armley, in 1913.

A well-known sight at their terminus at the bottom of Cookridge Street, Sammy Ledgard's 'blue wonders' were renowned for their 'family' atmosphere (which sometimes extended to the point where it was difficult to tell the conductor from the passengers). Here is a group of the company's vehicles at their Armley depot and the selection of registration numbers underlines another Ledgard trend: they bought buses from all over the place and every single one seemed different. But they endeared themselves to the travelling public, so much so that the *Yorkshire Evening Post* offered readers die-cast models of one of them in a recent promotion.

Those who have suffered grievously from ever-changing timetables, late buses, no buses, fume-belching buses and the need to travel into the city from far-flung housing estates to where an older generation had been removed from inner city back-to-backs, might well utter the words 'Those were the days' at the sight of this picture taken from the daffodil-clad embankment across the road from Leeds Central Bus Station. At that time Leeds Corporation Transport ruled supreme. One of the latest single-deck railcars glides quietly and cleanly toward York Road behind an older model which, too, will shortly break away from other road traffic to rattle off along the central area reserved for trams.

A veritable herd of LCT double deckers occupies the bus station, but on this fine spring day many of the folks living beyond the buses, in Quarry Hill Flats – Europe's largest block – will not be worried about transport; many of these inner-city dwellers would normally walk to work.

Trains a-plenty

While the Stockton & Darlington and Liverpool & Manchester railways were still over the horizon, Leeds had a form of railway. An Act of Parliament of 1758 authorised the building of a waggonway between the Manor of Middleton, south of the town, 'to supply the inhabitants of the town of Leeds with coals for their use and consumption'. Charles Brandling, of Gosforth Hall, near Killingworth, had experience of wooden waggonways on Tyneside and his inheritance of estates and collieries at Middleton put him on the road to fame and fortune.

His double-track line from Middleton to Casson Close, near Leeds Bridge, is shown in part in this engraving, with Christ Church behind the coal staiths. This pioneer line, to a gauge of 4ft 1in, was converted to standard gauge in 1881 and established another record when it became the first standard gauge line to be successfully preserved by amateurs, the Middleton Railway Preservation Society running its first train on 20 June 1960. Much development has been done on the line which is a popular attraction with enthusiasts and members of the public alike.

Members of the Middleton Railway Trust in 1969 with what was their latest acquisition – a diesel locomotive built by Hudswell Clarke, of Leeds. It started work 23 years earlier at Keighley gas works. As with their various rolling stock purchases, it was given a complete overhaul and put into service.

A turn-of-the-century day at Cross Gates Station. As the trim and well-polished little engine blows off steam over the clerestory-roofed coaches (probably lit by gas at that time), an important-looking city gent confers with the driver. The porter, almost as sharply dressed as the gent, has an assistant with him to handle what is well and truly a 'cart load' of luggage. Ladies flutter hither and thither while a blade in a boater strikes a nonchalant pose by the roof pillar. It could almost be a scene from a British film. But it is for real!

In 1921 the entrance to the old Wellington Station was in City Square, at the end of Wellington Street, with the old Queens Hotel on the left. The 'crack' trains for London ran from Central Station, on the site where the Royal Mail building stands today in Wellington Street. It was shared by various companies over the years, but latterly by the London and North Eastern Railway (LNER) and the London Midland & Scottish (LMS). The picture appears to have been taken in the years soon after World War Two, judging by the style of cars and the fact that the YMCA Forces Canteen appears to be still operating in the station building. A Brylcreem poster on the hoardings features a sailor – strange, considering that RAF types were more closely associated with that product! Dalton's Cereal Flakes were still in business, and some of those splendid holiday posters were starting to appear again. The station concourse was reached by the ramp which ran up from Wellington Street, past the side of the Great Northern Hotel (now the Wellesley), just off to the left of the picture.

And here is that concourse, with at least one passenger's luggage displaying a sticker for a sea voyage. *The Lady* magazine was priced at one shilling and most London expresses started from the platforms over to the left.

In 1937, the old Wellington and Leeds (New) Stations were rebuilt as Leeds City Station and came nearer than almost any other in Britain to having the sort of elegant concourse with a 'gate' system to platforms that was becoming typical of the big railway stations in the US. It had style, and the delights of the new Queens Hotel could be reached directly from the area. When this picture was taken down at Holbeck Motive Power Depot, British Railways' cleaners were hard at work on locomotives of the former LMS that would haul the great expresses away from 'city'. By then their British Railways livery was begrimed and it would not be long before the huge concrete coal bunker on the right would be as obsolete as the steam locomotives themselves.

Shush – it's the 'Hush Hush'! That was the name given by railwaymen to the LNER's No. 10,000, one of the most unusual locomotives ever to run in Britain, This historic shot was captured at Leeds City Station. The ancient, double running-board coach behind the tender hardly matched the smooth lines of the engine which had emerged from Darlington Works in 1929. The locomotive was something of an experiment which failed. Its unique, high-pressure water tube boiler proved unsatisfactory in service and eventually the engine was rebuilt at Doncaster in more conventional form.

No. 45705, *Jubilee* Class 4-6-0 *Seahorse* puts up a powerful screen of smoke and steam as it gets into its stride at Leeds City West Box on its way to Morecambe.

Not exactly the Inner-City style, but a valuable inter-provincial towns service: an ex-LNER 4-6-0 in the British Railways' livery gallops through Marsh Lane on a York-bound train from Leeds. The chimney betrays the fireman's handiwork as it approaches the climb up Marsh Lane cutting, part of which used to be Richmond Hill tunnel in the days of the original Leeds and Selby Railway.

Before train spotters became the target of cheap jibes from comedians whose main line is sex jokes, and not-in-the-real-world London newspaper columnists who find some curious connection between anoraks and train spotters, there was some measure of respect for youngsters who actually 'found something to do' and took part in a hobby which was preferable to vandalising and stealing cars, spray-painting anything or anybody, and beating-up the odd old lady *en route*. Needless to say, such remarks are not passed about anorak-wearing wrestlers, of which there are several!

So this magnificent study of the railway entrance to Leeds Central Station marks a site that would have been a mecca for spotters. Class A3 No.60112 *St Simon*, gets a final check before leaving for London, while Class J50 0-6-0 tank engine No.68988 shunts in the background. On the left is the huge 'tranship' goods station of the London Midland ami Scottish Railway (LMS) which stood on the ground where today's Aireside Centre is located. Almost everything else in this picture, which was on a series of viaducts and embankments, has also been razed down to that Ievel.

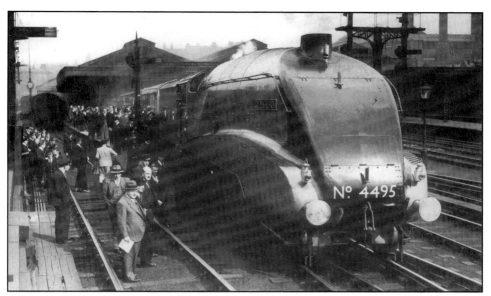

A crowd of LNER officials, well-wishers and train enthusiasts was at Central Station on 23 September 1937 to see streamlined A4 Pacific No.4495 *Golden Fleece* (formerly *Great Snipe*), ready to leave on a demostration run of West Riding Limited.

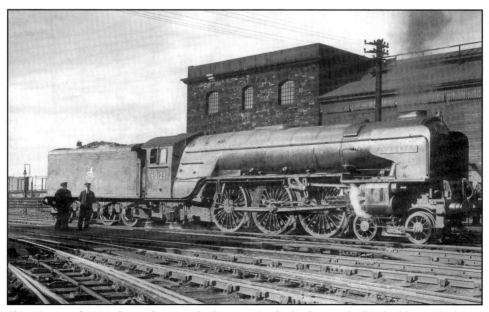

This picture of 1951 shows the stone-built tower in the background. This building, which was believed to be under a preservation order but appears increasingly derelict, is one of two which appear in the historic second picture in the introductory chapter of the book. Sadly, the purposeful-looking H.A. Ivatt engine of the LNER's A1 Class, with their famous off-beat exhaust, has gone the way of most metal.

A fascinating collection of rolling stock, much of it wooden, is scattered across this scene. The nose of an express locomotive is emerging from the shed on the right and there are some interesting and very old coaches in the middle distance. This was the Copely Hill Depot and most of the property has long since vanished from the area of that cat's cradle of roads which descends upon the gyratory built to sort out traffic from Armley, Wellington, Gelderd and Whitehall Roads approaching central Leeds.

Looking at this magnificent array of vintage signals, one can only wonder how the footplate crews of yesteryear, peering through smoke and steam on a murky night, ever figured-out which one was set for them! Here, York-based V-2 Class No.60843 passes Neville Hill with a Newcastle–Leeds train in May 1953. Nothing remains of the signals, engine, or its coaches.

The fireman, wearing clogs, pauses in his task of 'oiling round' a somewhat grimy Class A4 – No.60029 *Woodcock*, which was 'on shed' at Copley Hill, Leeds.

Resplendent in the fresh paint of the then new British Railways' express passenger engine livery, A1 Class No.60120 *Kittiwake* glistens at Wortley.

Plane Tree Hill to International Airport

What would become Leeds Bradford International Airport began as a sparse flying field at Yeadon (hard by 'Plane Tree Hill'), following the acquisition of the land by Leeds and Bradford Corporations in 1930. An early arrival there was Prince George, who landed on 13 July 1931, in a Gypsy Moth aircraft piloted by Captain H.V. Worrall, a Fiji-born instructor with the Yorkshire Aeroplane Club, who was later to make a chance remark that created the opportunity for the airport to grow into what it is today. The 'aerodrome' was officially opened in October that year and was soon popular with flying club members, as pictured here. Thc houses on the left were among the first structures to go in developments that have gone on ever since that time.

The 'Municipal Hangar', on the left, was the venue for that chance remark by Captain Worrall who was packing away the belongings of the Aeroplane Club in 1939 when Sir Roy Dobson, of A.V. Roe, later to become Chief Executive of the Hawker Siddeley Group, walked in and said he had been asked by the Ministry of Aircraft Production to find a site in Yorkshire for a 'shadow factory' where bombers could be built in comparative safety. He said he had been told to look at Doncaster and Yeadon.

'Why bother going to Doncaster?' asked Captain Worrall, a World War One Royal Naval Air Service pilot, who later flew Lawrence of Arabia around the Middle East. Sir Roy did not bother and the result was the giant factory which still stands to the north of the airport. Hundreds of Lancaster bombers were built there, also Avro Ansons, one of which is parked before the camouflaged hangar. The smaller building was the club house and site of the airport's control tower in its early days as Yeadon Aerodrome. Picture via Gerald Myers and courtesy of Mr R. Marshall.

This large wooden propeller was found at the works of Hustlers, of Yeadon, and presented to Yeadon Aviation Ltd., by the managing director, Mr W.D. Coustol. It was one of two which were fitted to the Blackburn Kangaroo, a Yorkshire-built twin-engined biplane with open cockpits which, in 1920, inaugurated the first-ever air service between Yorkshire and Holland. On one trip to what would later become Schiphol (Amsterdam) Airport, the Kangaroo made a 'dicky' landing and ploughed through a building site and over a railway line before coming to a halt. The restored propeller was later hung in the passenger hall at Leeds Bradford Airport.

The winter of 1963 was similar to the one we experienced in 2010–11, in terms of weather conditions. But Colonel Vivario, Chief de Cabinet, Belgian Ministry of Defence, had no qualms about ordering the pilot of his Belgian Air Force DC-4 Skymaster to land at Yeadon...whatever the weather. It was the first visit to Yeadon by an aircraft of this type.

The reason for Colonel Vivario's visit was something of a mystery, but BKS Air Transport soon rustled-up some steps and the worthy colonel (extreme right), his son (extreme left) and Madam Vivario were escorted to a waiting car on the snowbound apron by the then Airport Commandant, Mr Geoffrey Seller (in uniform).

Leeds-Bradford moved into thc turbo-prop era in 1961 when BKS Air Transport, the first airline to establish a successful network of services between Yorkshire, Northern Ireland, Eire and the Continent in addition to domestic services, put five Avro 748s to work. They were an immediate success and popular with passengers, particularly on the London (Heathrow) service.

The late Harry Fletcher, a *Yorkshire Evening Post* photographer who always had an eye for a different picture (he once put a stuffed fox under a hedge over which members of a famous Yorkshire hunt were to jump), had a split-second chance to catch this BKS Viscount landing on the Horsforth end of Leeds-Bradford's then newly extended main runway. On the skyline are the Cookridge communications and water towers; as for all those houses in the foreground, compare the scene with the view across Cookridge elsewhere in the book when none of them existed.

The arrival of this Douglas DC-7C *Baltic Sea* on 4 June 1965 caused near-hysteria among Yeadon's plane-spotting fraternity. It was then the largest aircraft ever to have landed at the airport. However, the uniformed figures were not the crew, they were members of a Dutch band due to play at several events in Yorkshire. But it was exciting. Why, the plane was even radar-equipped (it says so alongside the door) and had various other gizmos that had not previously been seen at Yeadon.

And here is another type: while the DC-7C was parked, a twin-engined Ambassador of BKS Air Transport was directed informally around the apron, its sausage-like shape emphasised, perhaps, by the prescence of a mechanic holding a carrier bag of a well-known local butcher.

The 1950s and 1960s seemed to be filled with inaugural flights of new air services here, there and everywhere. Aviation correspondents were barely back from one exhausting series of jet-lagged booze-ups and museum tours before they were off on another. Here some of the industry's finest are seen in the old aeroplane club-cum-terminal at Yeadon, being briefed on the forthcoming launch of Aer Lingus's Leeds-Bradford to New York service or, more accurately, Dakota or Fokker Friendship to Dublin, then by way of Boeing 707 to New York via Shannon and/or Boston.

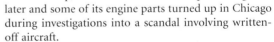

On 4 November 1984, the author won a long-time bet with Gordon Dennison, then Managing Director oi Leeds-Bradford Airport, that he would be the first person to step from a Boeing 747 Jumho jet on to the airport's apron.

Having gone to London to fly north in a 747 (aptly named Spirit of Yorkshire for the day), which he had chartered from British Airways on behalf of *Yorkshire Post* Newspapers, the author won his bet: but Mr Dennison turned the tables by having him met hy a sparsely dressed 'kissogram' girl who quickly brought him down to earth!

Some 800 *Yorkshire Evening Post* and *Yorkshire Post* readers flew on two round the north of England trips in the Spirit of Yorkshire that day, and countless thousands crowded every vantage point for miles around to see Captain Mike Webster, whose parents lived in Leeds, take the Jumbo on some (approved) low passes over the area. Sadly the Spirit of Yorkshire was destroyed after landing in Kuwait at the start of the Gulf War. Blown up, and reduced to near scrap, it was 'got at'

later and some of its engine parts turned up in Chicago during investigations into a scandal involving written-off aircraft.

Among the passengers on the Jumbo during one of its Leeds-Bradford flights was 84-year-old Mrs Margaret Bairstow who, until that day, had never even been inside an aircraft, having said she was 'petrified' of flying.

After a glass of champagne over the Irish Sea, and a conversation with Captain Webster, she left the aircraft asking: 'May I come back and have another flight, soon?'

She was born at Well Lane, Chapel Allerton on 9 July 1900 and her parents were typical of the country folk who had come to live in Leeds in search of better rewards and conditions. Most of her relatives were North Riding farming folk and she has many happy memories of childhood holidays at Carthorpe, near Ripon.

EDUCATION IN LEEDS

Founded in 1552 by William Sheafield, Priest of the Clarell Chapel in the Parish Church, Leeds Grammar School moved in 1624 to 'a pleasant field on the outskirts of the town'. That was roughly between the present line of Vicar Lane and the Grand Theatre and it remained there for nearly 300 years. This is the original building which was eventually used as an iron foundry following the school's move to the present building, near Woodhouse Moor, in 1859.

Another – and rather sorry view of the school from the other side, possibly taken at the time when demolition work was about to start, around 1898, for there is an excavation along the full length of the building.

Only the model of car in the foreground gives a clue as to when this picture was taken of the oldest part of the present Leeds Grammar School, work on which began in 1858.

Taken at Blenheim Primary School around 1906, this picture includes Cecil Brook Bairstow (fifth from the left with white frill collar, middle row) who became a highly successful Leeds publisher, producing books and brochures for local authorities, hotel and entertainment groups and other organisations all over Britain. Several pictures from the collection of the late Mr Bairstow are printed in this book. This is one of three which span three generations of his family (also see next photograph). He had a life-long interest in shipping and joined the Royal Navy under age on 23 February 1915, and was one of the youngest sailors at the Battle of Jutland the following year.

A different age, different dress…but similar anxious looks, cheeky looks, wry smiles and nervous smiles, although the members of this class at Cookridge Primary School in the early 1960s are more used to saying 'cheese' than the children in the previous picture, The late Mrs Bairstow's granddaughter, now Mrs Suzanne Brown, is fourth from the left in the second row. Her grandmother, Mr Bairstow's widow, appears in the 'Planes' section of this book.

Serious education for girls in Leeds began about 120 years ago. A group of women members of the Leeds Ladies' Educational Association and the Yorkshire Ladies' Council of Education decided to 'establish and maintain a High-Class Day School for Girls of Leeds which shall be to them what the Grammar School is to their brothers'. And so, under the ornate eaves of a rambling ivy-covered house in Woodhouse Lane, the academic future of the first 42 pupils of Leeds Girls' High School took its first faltering steps in 1876.

The roots of Leeds University go back to the Yorkshire College, whose Baines Wing is shown in 1895. Founded in 1874, the establishment gained full independence as Leeds University in 1904. Its most striking architectural feature today remains the impressive Parkinson Building which stands out well on the skyline and is immediately recognisable from many parts of the city.

More serious faces and one ncar-yawn: Group IV at Bramley Infants, date unknown, but almost certainly soon after the turn of the century.

'JIMMY'S' HOSPITAL AND THE LGI

The line up of the 'medical and the military' at James's during World War One reveals a fine body of men and women – and the inevitable pet dog towards the left of the front row.

A less formal picture (perhaps matron was on leave) of nurses among the lupins reveals some bonnie lasses among the staff of 1919. The picture appcared originally in a pictorial history of St James's, produced to mark the diamond jubilee of the hospital being given that name (it was previously the Leeds Union Infirmary).

Nearly 50 years later, this group of latter day 'Florence Nightingales' posed for a photograph on a fire escape of what was to become better known throughout the land as 'Jimmy's'. They had good reason to smile; they had just been given the news that they had qualified as registered nurses.

Only the two cars in the foreground give some idea of the date when this picture was taken of St James's Hospital.

This picture is a reminder that times were even tougher, even as recently as the 1920s. A close study of the faces of these inmates of the Beckett Street Workhouse, at St James's Hospital, tells a thousand stories. Even a politician raised on a diet of sound bites might be stopped in full flow.

The LGI, as most Leeds folk refer to 'their' infirmary, was known as the 'New Infirmary' at the time of this picture, in 1880. The author, who spent some time in one of the wards on the right at a much later date, feels the view has not changed all that much: but prefers it from outside rather than inside!

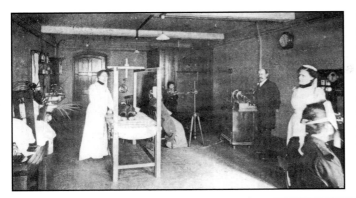

It is 1899 and in the X-Ray room of Leeds General Infirmary every modern convenience is on hand: electric light, central heating, two fragile X-Ray devices and a contraption which looks as though it was designed by Heath Robinson.

Now here is a familiar scene: the picture was taken at the turn of the century but this ward, or a near identical one did not appear to havc changed very much when thc author was in the LGI for a week in 1989. Thc furnace had gone, and there was vinyl floor covering. Those delicate beams, which looked as if they had been designed for a Lancashire and Yorkshire Railway bridge, had vanished, so had the aspidistras, and

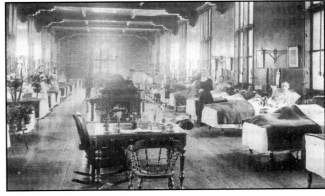

there were some new chairs. But the window blinds, or what was left of them, seemed familiar on looking at this picture. In 1989 the 'air conditioning' had not advanced much on the 1900 model: i.e. on those hot August nights we went out and sat on the fire escape in our pyjamas, envying the folks whooping it up in The George pub across Great George Street.

Meanwhile, modern air-conditioning is no respecter of old and rare photographic slides hence, we suspcct, the cracks on this picture of the now demolished Leeds Medical School in Park Stret (the

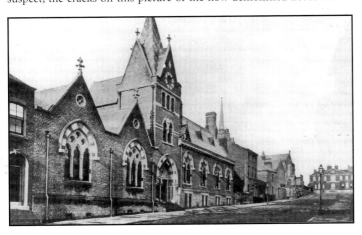

road with the Magistrates Courts). The school opened in 1865 and became a part of the university in 1884. Later, when the school moved to Thoresby Place, this building was used by thc specialist and highly-reputable firm of Thackeray's, the surgical instrument makers. It is now the site of the West Yorkshire Police Bridewell.

105

CHURCHES

Practically every building except the Parish Church has been long gone from Kirkgate, where Percy Robinson made this sketch on an unknown date. But the cart tracks among the cobbles reveal the hard use to which the road was put, leading to its clearance and widening before many more years had passcd. It was also spanned by a railway bridge at roughly the point where hc made his drawing.

Viewed from a slightly different angle, on what some might have described as 'a typical raw Leeds day', this photograph shows that the trams had advanced into Kirkgate, and the wind was blowing out of the south.

A 1904 view of the old St Anne's Cathedral which faced down Park Row. In 1901 it was bought for £46,000 by Leeds Corporation for road-widening, and replaced by the present cathedral some 100 yards or so further north, and facing on to Cookridge Street. It was opened in 1904. The original cathedral was completed in September, 1838, the first stone having been laid on 8 August 1837. The opening was on 24 October 1838.

A photograph fit to bring a sigh from anyone who faces the daily horror of Headingley's traffic...the clock of St Michael's Church, whose location and steeple are known to cricket fans the world over, says it is 5.30. And the doors of the Skyrack Inn (on the right) will have just opened for business, bringing a sigh of relief to the waiting customers. Sight of that clock always brings a memory to the author who, some years ago, was sitting amidst a crowd of robust Aussies at a Headingley Test Match before the days of pubs being open all day. As the clock struck three, a Sydney wag bellowed to Greg Chappell, at the wicket: 'For God's sake keep it going, Greg, these Pommie pubs don't open again 'till half-past five!'

A much-respected haven for the homeless, St George's Church, near the infirmary in Great George Street, was completed in 1838. Its crypt became famous throughout the land in the 1930s when the Revd Don Robins opened-up the area and developed it as a hostel for homeless men. Furniture was sparse, but they welcomed the soup and bread and a chance of a night's sleep on a hard bench. Thankfully, the work continues today

and facilities have been extended to meet the demand. Originally, the church had a 160ft spire, but this was blown down in the gales of 1962.

Park Square, between Westgate end and St Paul's Street, provides a haven of lunchtime rest from the lunacies of pressure placed upon workers in some surrounding offices. At one time it also had this church – St Paul's – on the south-east corner. Completed in 1793, and set to dominate the fashionable Georgian residential area, it was demolished in 1905 as much of the surrounding area was cleared. It would have been a sorry blow to over 1,000 people who worshipped in its large interior, many of them being seated in extensive galleries which gave an unrestricted view of the altar.

St Margaret's Church, Horsforth, stands as well today as it did in this long gone view. If only its stonework could be restored to its original shade! But what of the rest? Church Road is no longer a country lane; the fields on the left are full of houses; the road itself buzzes with traffic day and night; the fields on the right have gone and Morrison's supermarket and car park have replaced part of them. Even in these days of 'hands off' automatic landings, there are some pilots, it would appear, who use St Margaret's heavenward pointing spire as a reference when they want to make a tight turn on 'short finals' for landing at Leeds-Bradford International Airport.

Another sketch by Percy Robinson, made in 1844, shows the happily still existing St John's Church, set in its peaceful churchyard off busy New Briggate. It dates from 1634, a turbulent time when the country saw very few new churches, and was built for John Harrison, the noted Leeds merchant and benefactor, who is celebrated in a striking memorial window in the church. The style is Gothic, but with contemporary furnishings that have left a marvellous 17th-century interior. The wonderful screen and pulpit, an almost complete set of benches and a Royal Arms, are all of the period.

CINEMAS AND THEATRES

Any theatrical worthy of the name played Leeds at some time or other. The names of the 'greats' were regularly up in lights and thousands of theatrical bills were plastered around the city and cards containing details hung in shops (many of whose owners got a couple of free tickets for the favour). Likewise, the cinemas did a roaring trade before television and fears of a yob-ridden city centre ruined the pleasures of a family night-out for thousands of citizens who now accept what purports to be all-round entertainment in the lonely, but comparative safety of their barricaded homes.

What a tragic come down from the time when people could travel into the centre on a well-ordered tram, enjoy a few drinks, then take in the show at the 'Verts' (City Varieties), the Empire, Theatre Royal, Grand Theatre, or see the latest 'pictures' at one of the several score cinemas scattered around the city. There was also dancing at the Mecca Locamo, the Majestic Ballroom, Mark Altman's, the Capitol at Meanwood or at the various other dance halls around town. Cars could be parked almost anywhere without any thought of vandalism or theft. Otherwise there were late night trains, trams and buses to get you home in safety...what else?

Those really were the days and the sooner politicians and others correct the trends that have seen them fade near away, the sooner they will find the feel-good factor that they, and the rest of us, desire so much.

'Mum, what's a fauteuils?' you can hear Little Johnny ask as he surveys the 'Pit Stalls – Grand Circle & Fauteuils – Balcony' signs on the superb canopy at the Empire Palace in 1903. Many of the patrons went there by open-top tram or hansom cab. The Empire Luncheon Rooms, just to the left of the canopy, is advertising Ham Teas for eightpence; Plain Teas for fourpence.

These pictures illustrate forcibly how modern planning and architecture was imposed on the old styles. This is the ornate façade of the Empire theatre, originally the Empire Palace, in Briggate, displaying a 'modern' canopy.

The bland face of an office building was to replace a vibrant theatre which had brought joy to 'Loiners' since 1898. Only the word 'Empire' survived on the arcade which replaced a theatre whose boards were trodden hy hundreds of performers, many of whom went on to stardom and the medium – television – which helped to kill the Empire and hundreds of other theatres amd cinemas throughout the land.

111

The Empire fell under the hammers amid drills of the demolition men in 1962. A hoarding advertising the theatre's final show – the pantomime *Babes in the Wood* starring Nat Jackley and Ian Wallace – had crashed on to the roof of the canopy and tears came to the eyes of passing citizens who had enjoyed years of happy shows, whether they sat in the stalls, circle or 'The Gods!'.

A sign on the Lands Lane wall of the Theatre Royal claimed it to be 'The Most Popular Theatre in Yorkshire', and many would entirely agree with that statement. Certainly it was famous for pantomime with Francis Laidler's productions of such shows achieving national fame. The one for the 1956–57 season, when this picture was taken, was *Queen of Hearts*. King Charles Croft, on the right, is now a part of the Schofield's Centre.

Originally specialising in news programmes, the Tatler cinema, in Boar Lane, later flirted with some risque Continental films. By today's standards they were tame. The author recalls sitting outside the lonny while members of the City's licencing committee watched the full length of *Bitter Rice*, starring Silvano Mangano. Would they let the public see it? I asked a worthy alderman as they adjourned. 'Appen', he replied, and then joined the Boar Lane throng.

The Scala, in Albion Place, was a popular venue for dancers and film-goers. It had a superbly sprung dance floor – put well and truly to the test twice a year at the Spring and Autumn Frolic events run by Leeds journalists.

Go to the pictures, enjoy a dance, or a meal – they were all available at the Majestic in City Square in the 1930s. The War Memorial in the foreground was later moved to the Garden of Remembrance in the Headrow.

Some of the earliest films shown in Leeds were at the Rialto Cinema in Briggate (replaced by a Marks and Spencer store). George Raft and Joan Bennett were appearing in the last week of the showing *Woman Tamer* when this picture was taken. And to follow: Will Hay in *Oh! Mr Porter*. And then...the 'sold' sign was up already.

Below: Looking up Lands Lane, with the Theatre Royal on the left and the back doors of the Scala Theatre and Ballroom on the right. As now, Lewis's block spans the top of the Lane in which Jaguars, Standard Vanguards and Humbers feature among the parked cars.

A PRIDE OF PUBS

At a time when 'marketing persons' are obsessed with the idea that the Great British Public must have 'theme' pubs – and are giving some pubs a new theme for the third or fourth time in the last 30 years ('They change their fronts even more than shoe shops,' said a well-known Leeds landlord), it is nice to know that there are some pubs in the city that have changed but little. The joke in the trade is that, having gone through several changes of theme, some pubs have been put back into a style that was there originally...not that any genuine punter is going to risk the watering-down effects of weeping in his beer at the thought of it all.

And look at the effect it is having on giving directions to strangers: it is no use the long-used-to-it 'Loiner' saying: 'Turn right at the Cock and Bottle'. Chances are that it is now called Patrick Rafferty's Irish Pint, or some such concoction. But no doubt people will be saying the same thing 100 years from now, for the wheel has a habit of turning full circle, leaving the marketeers and whiz-kids hanging from the top.

So enjoy a whiff of the bar rooms of days gone by.

You will not have to look too carefully to establish a sporting connection between the caps of these gallant lads and the location of the Butcher's Inn. It was in Elland Road and Mr R. Archer, of Larkhill View, Leeds, who sent us the picture, knows that because the pub was owned by his grandfather, George Henry Archer. He used to brew beer on the premises and is pictured fifth from the right on the back row with, as ever, a flower in his lapel.

Another pub, another game: it is the outside of the Greyhound Inn in York Road, Leeds, headquarters of the Leeds Rugby Supporters' Club and the lads were celebrating after their annual trip to Wembley in 1936. Leeds beat Warrington 18–2 in that Final – which probably explains why the fans have the trophy before them.

A far cry from the large building which now bears its name, the Queen's Arms in Harrogate Road over half a century ago was on the other side of the road. A coaching inn in the 18th century, it was on the route of the turnpike road from Leeds to Harrogate. Margaret Suttenstall, of Oakwood Park, Leeds, who supplied the picture, said it was a copy of one owned by Mrs Renee Firth, of Woodland View, who for several years lived in a flat in the converted inn.

The early 1920s are pin-pointed by Mr G. Stuart White, of The Drive, Cross Gates, as the time when this picture was taken, because Temple Newsam golf course had been laid out. Proof of this is in the notice on the right of the pub which reads: 'Try one here. Nearest house to the golf course.' Later, a new Irwin Arms was built to the right of this structure.

The Bull and Butcher was in Water Lane, Holbeck, and Mrs Dorothy Callaghan, of West Park, Leeds, supplied this photograph which shows her grandparents, Joseph (with children) and Mary (in doorway). The couple had nine children, seven of them girls and the one in the picture is Dorothy, after whom Mrs Callaghan was named.

The east side of Leeds used to be full of pubs. 'There's one at every street end,' they said of York Road, and the proof of the statement was there when hundreds of houses were demolished in that area but many pubs remained. The Silkmill Inn was in Mill Street, in the 'Old Bank' district – 'Where the bobbies were always in pairs,' said a one-time resident. Christine Golton, of Harehills, Leeds, who supplied the picture, said it was taken in 1918 when the locals were celebrating the end of World War One. The pub was owned by the Butler family, who brewed their own beer. Christine's late father, a small boy at the time the picture was taken, is sitting on the kerb ('causer-edge' in those days), second from the left.

Holbeck Carnival was always a good excuse for dressing up and these customers of The Old Blue Ball in 1921 certainly made a day of it. Proceeds were in aid of a nurses' charity. The lettering on the wall to the left may be puzzling, under a magnifying glass the legend becomes Sparkling Ale Special.

All set for a day trip, and if you had not got an umbrella you could always wear a large flat cap, this group of worthies was outside the Spring Hill Tavern in Buslingthorpe Lane.

While its owner drank inside, the horse with the carriage took a drink from a trough outside the New Inn, Dewsbury Road, which stood near the tram terminus. The 1960 edition of *The Huntsman*, the Joshua Tetley house magazine in which the picture appears, also records that the pub was altered in 1908 and again in 1927. It was popular with Hunslet RL fans.

We have looked at a few pubs, but McConnell's was something else. In Briggate, near the Market Street Arcade, it advertised 'old world bars' and it was a cross between something out of Dickens and a Wild West saloon, with sawdust on the floor amid huge vats behind the bar. Mrs D.H. Atkinson, of Montagu Crescent, Leeds, who supplied the picture, said: 'When my husband and I were courting, he took me to McConnell's. There was no comfort, one sat on barrels and there was an extremely long bar. The beer, which was superb, could only be bought in half pints.' Tell 'em that down 'unslet.

Six pubs around the Westgate area of Leeds disappeared in the early 1970s, most of them because of the land needed for the Inner Ring Road flyover and its associated entry and exit roads. Two that stood on Westgate itself were the Leeds Arms and Fisherman's Hut.

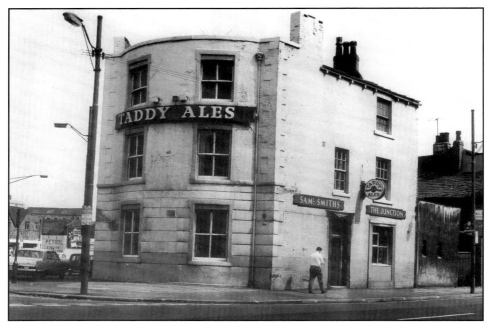

On the corner opposite the Fairburn Lawson building, which stood on the corner of Wellington Road and Kirkstall Road, there was the Wellington Inn and, a few hundred yards further along Kirkstall Road was The Junction. On the last night of the Wellington's life, the landlord invited regulars to turn up and 'drink the pub dry'. They did.

On the other side of Wellington Bridge, at the junction with Armley Road, was the White Horse, also a victim of the new road plans. Traces of the car showrooms (on the right) still remain.

The North Eastern, not far from the old Salvation Army property on Wellington Street, was popular with all classes of society; not least the journalists, commercial and printing staffs of *Yorkshire Post* Newspapers. Not only was the beer good, it served some of the best 'bap' or teacake sandwiches in the area. Its demolition was one of the fastest jobs performed in the city – some newsmen who had been drinking there on a Friday night swore they returned to work on the Monday to find it flattened! Mysteriously, the then editor of the *Yorkshire Evening Post* came into possession of the only known souvenir – a brass bell which used to stand on the bar to attract the landlord's attention. Maybe his attention wandered that last night...

A chapter dealing with pubs in Leeds would not be complete without special mention of a name more closely associated with brewing in the city than any other, Joshua Tetley. Although the company has seen many changes over the past 30 years, not least in relation to the style and naming, or renaming, of some of its pubs, the name Tetley (or more often 'Tet's' with old Loiners) is the one likely to come to mind first when the name of the product is linked with Leeds. And the company's sports sponsorship has ensured that the name Tetley is well known 12,000 miles from Leeds Bridge as are most of the world's top international beers. Looking at the brewery site today, it is a far cry from this humble brewhouse scene of the 1870s. Picture: Joshua Tetley Collection.

The skills required to produce barrels for Tetley beer were honed in this cooper's shop at the brewery. Today they are demonstrated in the superb Tetley's Brewery Wharf project, a £6 million visitor attraction which was voted winner of the 'Best Newcomer to Tourism' section of the Yorkshire and Humberside Tourist Board's White Rose Awards in 1995. Picture: Joshua Tetley Collection.

Pictured in the Woodhouse area in 1936 is Mr Jim Wilson, a member of a Tetley distribution crew, whose round covered the off-licence shops in the district. He had joined the company at the age of 21 and his horse, 'French', worked around Woodhouse until he left to fight for King and Country in 1941. The particular shop to which he was delivering was situated in Kingston Road, off St Mark's Road, and the children on the horse were those of the shop's owner. Jim returned to Tetley's after the war and worked in the transport department until he retired in 1973. Picture: Joshua Tetley Collection.

Both Clifford Lackey, and his successor as Public Relations Manager Colin Waite, found that the Tetley shire horses were one of the best publicity advantages available to the company, because of their immense popularity. They appeared (and still do) on the brewery's calendars, at countless shows, presentations, galas and what-have-you. Here they are leading the 'Parade of Transport down the years' which formed apart of the *Yorkshire Evening Post's* 90th birthday celebrations. They went to Spain and stole the show at the 'Festival of the Horse' in Jerez, and an American airline executive, born in Yorkshire, flew here to sing their praises in a BBC radio broadcast.

Without doubt, the man who did much to steer the Tetley horses to fame was the late Albert Hobson, long-time head horseman with the company. One of Yorkshire's great characters, he was a stickler for detail, especially when it came to the turn-out of 'his 'osses'. Harness was polished, brass shone, no sergeant major ever made closer kit inspections. Here he is with a 'ton or two' of his favourite animals. Brewery horse people, and others, came from all over Britain to his funeral. Picture: Joshua Tetley Collection.

More years ago than the author cares to remember, a threat to take horsedrawn traffic off the streets of Leeds led to a public outcry, with Tetley fans in the vanguard. The *Yorkshire Evening Post* joined them and the result produced the biggest ever postbag of letters to the newspaper, saying that the Tetley Shires must be allowed to stay on the streets of the city. The threat was withdrawn, but the

YEP continued its long-time association with Tetley's through various promotions. In due course the brewery company sought to thank a newspaper 'which so closely represented Leeds and its citizens', and also reflected the attitude of Tetley's in that respect. The result was a decision to name one of its shires after *Yorkshire Post* Newspapers' Promotions and Publicity Manager, and here he is with 'his' horse, wearing the family name on a specially-made brass plate. On a subsequent occasion, Albert Hobson was asked by a Leeds journalist how the horse was coming along. The tongue-in-cheek reply was typical of Albert: 'He's as daft as him he's named after,' he quipped. Sadly, Rowley (the horse) also departed for the great grazing ground in the sky in the 1990s, but his picture in retirement in a field near Ripon has a special place in the author's home.

ROYAL OCCASIONS

7 July 1908 brought out the troops in force, but with the best of intentions, when King Edward VII and Queen Alexandra visited the city. This huge throng was outside the Town Hall to witness their departure. Perhaps the staff in the windows at Mosleys, a famous Leeds name, were as keen to spot any of their 'customers' in the crowd as they were to give the King and Queen a rapturous welcome. Mrs Margaret Bairstow, of Roumlhay, who is mentioned in the 'Planes' section of this book, recalls watching the King and Queen pass by in their royal carriage from a window above the parade route.

While the King and Queen prepared to move off to the university, the statue of the late Queen Victoria, who had seen it all before, countless times, remained aloof and dignified above the general proceedings.

King Edward VII and Queen Alexandra riding in the state carriage as they leave Leeds University on their tour of the city.

The montage of pictures on this postcard, issued to mark the visit, shows clockwise from the top: the City Boundary Arch at Moortown; the date of the event; the Royal Party *en route* to Moortown for the farewell ceremonies; The Lord Mayor (Sir W.L. Hepton), Lady Hepton and Miss D. Hepton returning to the city.

That night the city was *en fête*, as they say in Gipton, and this electric tram, decorated with 3,000 illuminated bulbs, was sent out to tour the system, to the delight of thousands of small boys and girls allowed to stay up late to see it.

A proud moment for officials of the Great Yorkshire Show on 13 July 1932 when the event was staged at Temple Newsam, during the days when it was something of a moveable feast. The then Duchess of York (the late Queen Mother), is pictured with the late George VI inspecting horses in the show ring. Lord and Lady Irwin are in conversation behind the Royal couple.

129

The following year, their Majesties King George V and Queen Mary were in the city to open the brand-new municipal headquarters, the Civic Hall. They also visited the Town Hall and are seen here on arrival. Compare this with the first picture of King Edward VII and Queen Alexandra's visit and you will note that the statue of Queen Victoria still sits in solitary state on its plinth, but the Leeds grime has blackened Oxford Place Chapel over the intervening years, and a number of trees have spoiled the view of the proceedings for Mosley's rent collectors. What is remarkable, on close examination, is the number of nurses among the guests on the Town Hall steps, a precaution, perhaps, in view of medical problems which arose around the time of the visit of the previous monarch and his queen.

Mrs Audrey Wakefield, of Kirkstall, took this photograph of the King and Queen leaving the Town Hall with her Box Brownie camera which cost 12s 6d (63p in today's money).

The then Lord Mayor of Leeds, Mr Tom Coombs, reading the proclamation of King George VI at Leeds Civic Hall on 15 December 1936.

On 26 April 1954, Her Majesty the Queen Mother attended a Civic Dinner at Leeds Civic Hall to welcome delegates to the Jubilee Celebrations of the University of Leeds. Here she is with the then Lord Mayor, Alderman D.G. Cowling, after the dinner.

The following day, HM The Queen Mother attended the university's Degree Ceremony at the Town Hall, accompanied by the then Princess Royal, Countess of Harewood, who was Chancellor of the University. They are pictured leaving the Town Hall for lunch at the Queens Hotel.

It is October 1958, and HM The Queen is arriving at Leeds Town Hall to attend the final concert of the Leeds Centenary Musical Festival. She was met by Lord Scarborough, then Lord-Lieutenant of the West Riding.

Seemingly, some confusion arose when the Royal party came to take their seats for the Festival performance of Handel's *Samson*. The lady with her back to the camera, who appears to have dropped what looks like a violin, is being assisted by the Earl of Harewood. Meanwhile, as ever, the Duke of Edinburgh looks around to se what is going on.

During the Centenary the Royal party met musicians who had taken part. Among them was top band leader Duke Ellington, seen chatting with the Queen. It is doubtful that she enquired how other Americans such as Count Basie and Earl Hines got their titles. But jazz fans treasure a memory of a visit to this country by Louis Armstrong who, learning that the then monarch liked a particular tune associated with the trumpeter, paused for a moment after a hot number, looked up at the Royal box and said: 'The next one's for you, Rex.'

MOVERS AND SHAKERS...

Horse vans were still being used for house removals when J.C. Kirby & Son introduced the latest motor transport. The solid tyres of this type of vehicle no doubt caused apprehensive housewives to use large amounts of packing to protect their best china from the 'shakes' induced by cobbled streets. Over the years many Leeds families 'flitted' via the Kirby vans. Originally the Kirby premises were in New Wortley. They later moved to Oldfield Lane. Green Lane Council School, with its famous rooftop playground, is on the left.

In an age of plain vans and lorries which many people feel should carry some sort of identification for all manner of reasons, it is good to see that the tradesmen of yesteryear had nothing to hide and, indeed, their vehicles were virtually 'mobile billboards'. A booklet from Mr John Cole, of Cookridge,

included this picture. The Cole family were removal contractors from 1878 and were involved with steam traction from 1904. The vehicle pictured is a 1917 Dennis ex-War Department lorry with a van body, as it was in 1931 when the booklet was printed.

William and Mary McManus, of Meanwood, had the sense to use a vehicle with balloon tyres when they sold ice cream from it at weekends and holidays in the 1920s. The converted Model 'T' Ford was a welcome sight for walkers from Meanwood Woods to Adel Church. The photograph came from Mr T. Suggit, of Silk Mill Drive, Leeds, grandson of William and Mary.

If doctors and engineers see fit to put letters behind their names, why not drain cleaners? Signs on the cart of E. Wooler & Son, RP (By Exam) MIP, Sanitary Engineers, told it all! Even the horse looks as if it was used to posing for pictures. The photograph came from Mr S. Skelton, of Horsforth, who served an apprenticeship with Wooler's plumbing firm in the 1950s.

FIRE BRIGADES AND FIRES

What locals then called 'The Great Fire of Leeds', in 1906, was a blaze at the Great Northern Hotel, later the Wellesley, along with Hotham and Whiting's premises in Wellington Street. At the scene was this steam-powered pump, with the flat-capped driver tending its own fire to power the pump while two firemen in splendid brass helmets stand-by. Picture courtesy of Mr Maurice Scott, of Cross Gates, a former member of Leeds Fire Brigade. According to a booklet published by the late Mr C.B. Bairstow, the Common Council of Leeds, in 1694, gave the sum of £40 'as an encouragement and in consideration of Henry Gillert, of Leicester and George Sorocold, of Derby, for laying an engine to convey water from the River Aire through the streets to all houses in the town of Leeds, who should wish to purchase the same of them and exempted them from taxes.' After improvements in 1754, 1790 and later years, water was pumped from the river into small reservoirs in New Street, St John's and Albion Street, at the rate of 80 or 90 gallons a minute. The Leeds Volunteers were created in 1794 and distinguished themselves 'by their spirited endeavours to preserve order' at various fires. Later, a number of insurance companies operated their own fire brigades but the first real progress towards a city brigade came in 1860 when the Watch Committee took over responsibility for the protection of the town from fire.

A fine body of men. Pudsey Corporation's Fire Brigade seem to be celebrating the winning of a trophy in the photograph which came via Mr W. Sharp, of Farsley. Whatever the occasion, it was a smart turn-out.

Perhaps the greatest fire in Leeds, certainly within living memory, was that at Leeds Markets in December 1975. Here are firemen at the height of the blaze, with sections of the roof collapsing in front of them.

Thc following morning thousands of people to whom the market was a shopping mecca, turned out to see the still smouldering wreckage, to check on whether or not their favourite stalls were still in business and commiserate with the shaken stall-holders.

Among the sympathetic visitors who subsequently visited the site was HRH The Prince of Wales who was quickly in among the wreckage, lending a sympathetic ear to all concerncd.

Nearly two thirds of the large 'rows' section of the market was destroycd. Fortunately, as this aerial picture taken the following morning shows the splendid old main markets building, beyond thc roofs of the 'rows' area, escaped much damage, although goods were affected by smoke and water. The Central Bus Station is in the bottom left-hand corner of the picture; the Corn Exchange near the top left-hand corner, with Millgarth Police Station bottom right.

INCIDENTS AND ACCIDENTS

'Ere, 'arry, shouldn't they give this chap a ticket for parking like that?' The driver of a Ford 'Pop' cases it under the tail plane of a Bristol Freighter which had been blown off the then Yeadon Airport apron and through the airport perimeter fence in a June gale in 1962.

Everyone concerned survived to tell the tale, and even laugh about it, after this British Midland Dakota, named *Dovedale*, came to grief at Leeds and Bradford Airport in February 1965. Workmen were completing concreting on a section of what was then the new main runway when this early morning Derby-Yeadon-Glasgow flight came in to land. There had been heavy rain during the night and it was still raining hard when the pilot touched down. When he applied the brakes, the DC-3 bcgan to 'aquaplane' on the wet runway and the empty oil drums which marked the end of the usable concrete were coming up fast. Almost at the moment the pilot realised he was not going to stop it, the unhappy concrete layers also realised it, and ran off in all directions, leaving footprints, the tyre marks of a Land Rover, planks, tools, and the full outline of one of them who fell, in the freshly-laid concrete! The captain had the sense to steer the aircraft to one side and it ran up an earth banking where the undercarriage collapsed and it sank on to the mud. There were some minor injuries and the clothes of everyone on board were ruined as they slithered away to the terminal. There, the author interviewed a Scottish passenger who had filled himself immediately with his homeland's favourite tipple in seconds flat and uttered the immortal words: 'I intend to complain to the Scottish aviation authorities. I have never once enjoyed landing here at Glasgow, ye ken!'

If you thought that prisoners gaining access to the roof of jails and hurling off slates was something geared to the 1990s, think again. Mr Eric Doyle, of Thornhill Place, Upper Wortley, was given this picture by his uncle, Mr William Bottom, many years ago. Believed to have been taken in the 1920s, it shows a row of local lads sitting on a wall across the road from Armley Jail as a chap who, quite obviously was not doing repairs, started hurling slates, to the fascination of the lads in the foreground.

Trams were stopped and other traffic had to be diverted when this World War Two-type Austerity steam locomotive ran away backwards and crashed through a boundary wall at Marsh Lane sidings,

Leeds. Residents of Quarry Hill Flats, on the left, had the best view. The heavily-laden coal tender landed upright in the roadway. The badly-damaged locomotive was left hanging perilously over the pavement. It was suspected that the engine had been deliberately set in motion but this was never confirmed.

Tram No. 281, on the Leeds and Pudsey route, became separated from the track at the junction outside Fred Coe's Blinds, Carpets and Curtains emporium and entered the shop in a most unusual fashion. There is no rceord of what happened to the driver, or of what Mr Coe said to him. But you can be sure he did not say: 'Have a nice day,' when he left.

Keeping a reasonably friendly eye on the proceedings are three Leeds bobbies with a group of what are described as 'helpers' in the Leeds Gas Strike of around 1912 or 1913.

If the Bosnian Serbs had mined the Headingley pitch thcy could have hardly caused more consternation than did the perpetrators of this 'international incident'. International because England were playing Australia in 1975 and during the night, wreckers campaigning for the release of George Davis, a London East-Ender serving 20 years for a crime they claimed he did not commit, partially dug-up the Test wicket and dumped oil on the turf. But they certainly did commit a crime for with England one down in the Test series, the home team were unable to secure the win they needed to help them regain the Ashes. Jack Hickes's picture shows Tony Greig and Ian Chappell, the English and Australian captains, examining the ruined wicket. They decided it was impossible for the match to continue at Headingley.

FROM VILLAGES TO SUBURBS

As described earlier, in addition to the then town of Leeds growing outwards from Leeds Bridge, there was a good deal of 'in-filling' as thc villages and hamlets which surrounded the town – on both sides of the River Aire – started to expand. But the villagers were a proud lot and, even today, some of them like to defend the names of their locations from 'predatory' Leeds; among them are Horsforth, Bramley, Shadwell, Hunslet and Cookridge. The latter suburb still retains a 'Cookridge Village' address for its local subpost office but what has happened to the area in the past 50 years can be apprcciated by examination of this photograph, taken in the late 1950s by Irving Crawford from his then home in Tinshill Road. The whole of the wooded area between the camera position to beyond the line of trees which runs practically all the way across the picture, is now built up and has the population of a moderately sized town. Most of the fields up towards the skyline above the roof of the house on the left of the picture have gone, and are now a part of the Scotland Lane estate. The large (and long) black building on the skyline to the right was the huge flight shed where Lancaster bombers and other aircraft built at the World War Two Yeadon 'shadow factory' (just to the right) were completed, or held for flight testing. The flight shed ended its days storing some 80,000 tons of fertiliser!

Leeds Bradford International Airport now occupies about half the skyline.

A million miles from the near-gridlock of today's city streets...this neat little bus stands at the Farnley terminus on a lovely summer's day. Picture from Miss O.M. Schofield's late father's collection.

Not the 'Deadwood Stage' but a grand old open-topped bus at the Shadwell terminus, ready to set out for Moortown. There was little weather protection for the driver – not even a windscreen. And even less for the top deck passengers. Picture collrtesy of Mrs W. Wilson, of Wetherby.

Road ragers eat your hearts out...a solitary horse and trap represent the total mobility of the hour when this picture was taken of Moortown, with St John's Church slumbering up on the left. No dual carriageways, twin roundabouts, proposed fly-overs, apartment blocks, car parks, Marks and Sparks or traffic lights. But heed to it, telcphone poles have appeared. Why, in some century to come, some lunatic might invent a hand-held telephone you could carry about with you in the trap! Some hope, let's get off to the Chained Bull...

Who does that Austin owner think he is – parking like that? There is a fine assortment of chimneys around the 'cop shop' in Harrogate Road, Chapel Allerton, as the tram conductor looks back to check if they have missed the badly parked car.

Sailor suits, adorable hats, a fashionable skirt and a queue to board the Hyde Park tram (via city centre) at the corner of Beeston Hill and Lady Pit Street. As ever, there is a daft dog watching it all from the corner and somebody's Malt Bread van is on its way to the next customer's house. And just look at the fancy wrought ironwork on that tram standard.

Time was when nearly every street corner in the (by then) heavily built-up red brick areas of Leeds could boast its corner shop. This newsagent's shop at 196 Kirkstall Road, was not actually on a corner but it was one of the best-known in what, not all that long ago, had been a village on the old waggon road that went out by the abbey. Taken in October 1911, our picture shows Mrs Emma Mitton in the doorway of the prcmises where her husband gave so much prominence to the *Yorkshire Evening Post.*

There was oilcloth shirts, bits of this and bits of that outside Deacon's shop in Town Street, Stanningly, and a good tram service when this picture was taken. And if the trams did not suit, a sign on the left shows the direction of the Great Northern Railway Passenger Station.

The start of the Farnley Grand Prix! Three vehicles share the wires at Moor Top, Farnley. The 'toast rack' single deck tram on the left is heading for the Corn Exchange, the 'trackless' trolley bus on the right will need to be shifted if the open-top double-deck tram behind is to get to Whitehall Road. And what was 'Nuholic' advertised on the tram? – it sounds like a plague. Closer examination reveals it to be a soap.

The worthy citizens of Guiseley do not look exactly overjoyed at the arrival of their first tram in 1909. It cannot have been the fare that disappointed them – it was only three old pence from Guiseley to Briggate. Perhaps they felt better when the track was extended to the White Cross and they could ride up for a pint. There used to be a chap in a local pub, which was nick-named 'The Swingers', who swore that at one time, apart from one stretch of half a mile near Todmorden, you could ride all the way from Leeds to Blackburn via the tramway systems of various companies amd local authorities. He was always good for a pint if you were prepared to agree with him!

When the trams reached Churwell, the locals could enjoy a much smoother ride into Leeds than they had been used to on the stone setts and cobbles on which the old horse buses used to run. Churwell Hill (pictured) provided some exciting rides and was also the scene of one of the worst tram accidents on the entire Leeds system. The photograph was found at the Half Way House Inn, at Morley, and kindly supplied by Mrs N.C. Wilson, of Churwell.

The River Aire tinkles along under Rodley's sweeping stone bridge as the locals perambulate with parasols. Sunday as it used to be.

The Fleece still stands, on the right, on Horsforth's New Road side. And the John Smith's tastes just as good as it did when this 70-year-old sign advertised Tadcaster's most famous product. How Horsforth's senior citizens must sigh for the days when you could cross the road without taking your life in your hands.

Woodhouse had lost its village status and was close to becoming an inner-city area when this tram clattered past what is now the Feast and Firkin pub at the edge of the moor, and overtook the Model 'T' Ford van on the right. The buildings of Leeds University's Department of Civil Engineering long ago replaced those on the left.

THE 'LUNGS' OF A CITY

To the surprise of visitors over the years – especially those from south of Watford – Leeds has been blessed with a good number of parks and open spaces. And for devotees of the small white ball, it has a plentiful supply of golf courses. Temple Newsam and Roundhay are among the largest park areas, and whilst the residents of East Leeds would stoutly defend all claims for the former, it would probably be fair to say that Roundhay is the most famous. It was purchased for the city in October 1871 at a total cost of £139,000. The previous owner was shipping magnate Thomas Nicholson. Its lakes, woods, bandstand bathing pool, arena, 'Hill 60', Mansion, formal gardens and great open areas have attracted millions to all-year-round activities, night and day. Pre-war military tattoos drew crowds from all over Yorkshire. The much-missed Children's Days, in which thousands of Leeds schoolchildren took part, were admired by and copied by education authorities all over the country. More recently, rock and pop concerts featuring international stars have had fans and participants from all over the world flying into Leeds Bradford International Airport. And heaven only knows how many dogs have been on more than nodding terms with every tree in the park. At the time of writing, plans were being mooted which might lead to the provision of funds to bring such places back to their former glory, with the idiocy of vandalism removed and families again able to fully appreciate and enjoy the facilities for which they and their forebears have contributed over the years.

Progress in the shape of a telephone pole had already intruded into the countryside city dwellers liked to visit when this picture was taken of what is believed to be a section of King Lane, near Adel Crags. The lady with the velocipede in the distance has, sensibly, removed herself from the contraption so as to walk safely down the hill.

The remains of an aqueduct that once carried the Leeds water supply from Eccup Reservoir to the filter beds at Headingley were visited by many Sunday afternoon walkers in Add Woods, and were known locally as the Seven Arches. The picture dates from about 1900, but the predecessors of Yorkshire Water had already seen fit to replace the aqueduct in 1866 with pipe lines, and a portion of pipe is seen on the left.

England's green and pleasant land...the parasols are out and the bandstand the centre of attraction on a Roundhay summer's day early this century.

Same place, but very obviously a different day. One of the park's lakes takes on a Lowry-like appearance – or is it one of the St Petersburg school? – when it froze in 1908.

It is summer now – a boatman, complete with boat hook and ticket machine waiting for trade by the park lake. In the background is the *Mary Gordon*, a powered yacht which plied the lake with parties of sightseers.

150

'I say...look at that photographer chappie setting-up his device down there. I don't suppose he could be going to...' Yes, he was, here is his charming turn-of-the-century study on the path leading up to the mansion. Thinks: could that be the original granny with the 'gamp' from Giles's famous *Daily Express* cartoons, sitting in front of the fountain?

Not Nüremberg, but the arena at Roundhay on 26 June 1927 with a full-scale physical training display by scores of schoolchildren when the children of Leeds were far fitter, thanks to an absence of television and computer games, and generally readily and happily supported by teachers, who put in countless hours to produce such precision. And there is an indication of family values in the huge crowd of mums, dads, grandparents, aunts, uncles and neighbours on 'Hill 60'!

The highlight of every Children's Day was the arrival of the Children's Day Queen. By the time it got to this stage, each year, successive queens had received as much attention from the local Press as would any visiting film star. And Women's Fashion Editors mopped their brows if their forecasts as to 'what she'll be wearing' proved right. In 1949, it was Joan Thompson, pictured, who was the centre of their attention.

Summertime... and the going is easy...'Don't worry, Clara, I used to row the admiral in one of these when I was with the old flotilla during the war.' The tales they used to tell on Roundhay Park lake!

East Enders; the name has vastly different connotations to residents of the east sides of the cities of Leeds and London. On the rising ground before coming to the glories of the great spread of the Plain of York, there is still a fair amount of open space, even after the building of huge housing estates. Amidst it all lies Temple Newsam House on land which The Knights Templar had acquired the Manor of Newsam in 1155. The house dates back to the 16th century. The late Lord Halifax, son of the former owner, and who spent part of his boyhood there, is pictured before the house on a visit in 1964. (His father, Lord Irwin, is pictured in the Royal Visits section of this book).

So, the East Enders of Leeds have much of which to be proud. And the East Enders of London's Limehouse, Bethnal Green and Shoreditch can be happy in the knowledge that they are highly unlikely ever to have open-cast coalmines within sight of their stately, or un-stately, homes.

Temple Newsam was purchased by the City of Leeds in 1922 and the official opening of what is now one of the nation's finest museums was on 19 October 1923, when this photograph was taken of the 'great and the good' who had been invited.

153

Supplied by Middleton historian Eddie Doherty, this picture was taken in 1910 and showed former cottages occupied by miners at the long defunct Venture Pit at Middleton. Part of the building on the left, where a woman and two children are standing in the doorway, later became part of Middleton Park Café.

'Keep still, you two. Your uncle wants to take your likeness...' An outing to Middleton Park Lake in 1910.

In 1934 nothing was quite like a trip to Golden Acre Park for the children of Leeds (and plenty more from surrounding towns and cities). For those without cars, it meant a healthy walk along Otley Road from the Lawnswood tram terminus, but bah gum, it were worth it! This aerial picture shows the layout with the miniature railway round the whole of the park. It had stations, bridges, viaducts – even a 'tunnel' just like the ones you could buy for Hornby trains. Some of Golden Acre's rolling stock is believed to have ended-up on the Blackpool Pleasure Beach railway in later years. Prominent in the picture are the popular boating lake and much-loved ballroom. The café (foreground) is one of the few surviving pieces of this famous pleasure park.

Nearer the city centre, Woodhouse Moor has hosted an annual 'Feast', various exhibitions and displays, many a circus, and the assembly area for the city's annual Lord Mayor's parade vehicles. It is also popular with university students and locals alike on summer evenings. Years ago, as a young journalist, the author was sent for by the late Mr R.W. Shawcross, then editor of the former *Yorkshire Evening News*, who said: 'Allen, I want you to go with a photographer to Woodhouse Moor and get a new angle on Chipperfield's Circus. I am tired of posed pictures of girls with horses.' At Woodhouse Moor, we were invited into the enormous and luxurious caravan of Mr Chipperfield, complete with stone fireplace. He listened, then said: 'How about a story on the oldest wire-walker in Europe?' Within minutes, the aforementioned wire-walker had been introduced to us and he said: 'Mister Rowley, how you like to try a ride across?' I was halfway up Otley Road before photographer Irving Crawford caught me and took me back and I was soon, literally, up the pole. On 4ft x 4ft square platform, swaying the wind, I climbed on to the back of this amazing pensioner and off we went. Was I apprehensive? Absolutely! But I concentrated on the thought that he looked rather like General Montgomery and sincerely hoped he was just as successful as the general in his efforts! A yard from the other platform, which was swaying about under the bulk of my longtime colleague, Irving, who, as folk used to say: 'enjoyed a good table', the veteran leapt forward and the three of us finished-up clutching each other like a family of monkeys. Back at the office, the editor appeared to go ballistic when he heard what we had done. 'Can you imagine the insurance claim on the paper if you'd fallen?'

he asked. Crestfallen, we were about to leave when he turned the other cheek and, with a wink, said: 'By the way, I propose to run the picture across five columns on page one.' And here it is, loaned by my colleague, Irving.

HARD TIMES, HAPPY TIMES...

The industrial revolution that helped to build the foundations of what is today a great and successful city brought in its wake a down side of conditions unimaginable to even those unfortunates who, today, have no hope of getting near the frame of the 'feel-good' factor, let alone inside it.

While there were good employers throughout Leeds and Yorkshire's industrial areas in general, who lent an ear to a desire for decent pay and conditions, there were many factories, mines, quarries, foundries and other areas of employment where they were little better off, all things considered, than those which prevail in some areas of the Far East today.

Strikes, lock-outs, hunger, misery and desperation were the lot of many. Fortunately, the 'help thy neighbour' spirit – without the need to actually love him – that developed amid the vast areas of back-to-back and terrace houses in the city proved to be a salvation for countless families. Unfortunately, some of what 'posh' folk called 'esprit de corps' was lost when such close-knit groups were moved to farflung housing estates and often split-up in the process.

A young Australian visitor, being driven along Kirkstall Road by the author a year or two ago, asked why it was necessary to have so many 'man-hole' covers along the highway. Told that rumour had it that each one represented the end of a street of back-to-back houses long gone, the Antipodean visitor, used to vast open spaces, asked: 'How did they stick it...?' The pictures in this chapter give part of the answer to that question.

In a cobbled back street of 'two-up, one-down and a cellar' houses, the children of miners involved in a lock-out are being fed soup and bread, and a drink, by kindly volunteers out to do what they can to help the innocent. The tables and food had been delivered by a van which had carried the poster left on the far wall reading: 'Children's Van of Help. Food, clothing and money wanted, please give us what you can spare.' There were not even enough benches for all the children to sit down, nor enough chairs in the houses. But those white smocks, and the shiny windows, are a credit to mothers determined to keep up appearances.

Folks complain today if the mechanical road sweeper misses their street on its (supposedly) regular run, but the grimness of this Dewsbury Road view strikes through as these lasses, employed as blouse hands, leave a local factory which looks about as cheerful as, well, you name it.

The road looks as if it has not been swept for months, the tram lines just visible through mud, pools of water, uneven cobbles and the inevitable 'horse muck'. No wonder they could not wait for summer to come around...And life was not exactly a barrel of laughs for the housewife. Here is Back Wood Street, Rodley, with women in full-length 'pinnies' and skins. There's a bit of 'in between' washing on a window-ledge, but it is not washday proper because there are no lines across the street from the outsize hooks on the walls of these homes. They also have boot-scrapers beside their doors and slide-up lids to their coal cellars under the windows. And if the coalman is the sort who leaves half his delivery on the 'causeway' (pavement), instead of shoving it down the cellar, guess who will have to do it; and sweep-up afterwards, then scour the front step clean? But at least, they will not have to worry about the microwave being set right or the tumble dryer, or automatic washer, or the clear-view electric oven and extractor, new shower head, central heating controls, taping a French cookery demo on TV, or whether to keep the bull bars on the four-wheel drive. What a relief that must have been!

When things improved, those who could afford it would enjoy a day out on a pub trip, like this one setting-out from the King's Arms (landlord W.C. Tempest) in Oewsbury Road, with a handful of women left behind to look after the pub.

It was not only 'the lads' who got the chance of a day out! This fine group of ladies was outside the New Inn, Town Street, Armley (at the bottom of 'The Gang'). Picture counesy of Mr Ernest Humphreys, of Town Street, Bramley, whose grandmother, Mrs Lucy Ellis, is seated third from left in the front row.

Five Whiffs of Leeds Air,
Makes you Frisky, Fresh & Fair.

While there were plenty of people glad to get out of the Leeds atmosphere for a day, there were others fascinated enough by city life to want to visit the place. This card is typical of those sold in the city. The message speaks for itself. It was posted by Mr Joseph Bairstow on 9 August 1912, to his mother who was on holiday at Sale Hill Farm, Camblesforth, near Selby. Card from the collection of the late Mr C.B. Bairstow.

It is those hats again: Ask for the 'Beulah' these days and most people would direct you to Tong Road, Farnley, and a large road-house-type establishment. But this picture from Mrs R. Rice, of Sutherland Avenue, Roundhay, is of another Beulah Inn – in Hunslet. It stood on the corner of Galway Street and Bewerley Street and behind it was Punon Street, where world-famed actor Peter O'Toole lived as a child, she says. The ladies pictured here were setting out for a day trip in 1912.

There were, of course, other ways of enjoying yourself – especially if you could not afford a carriage, or more likely a 'chara'. Mr Ned West, a sprightly 80-year-old, who lived within a stone's throw of the White Cross Inn at Pudsey for some 72 years, was one of the team which erected this flagpole outside the pub in 1926. That is Ned, standing at the back next to the pub's first license, Anhur Scot (the only gent not wearing a cap). He recalled that the pole was about 30ft tall and it was greased before being erected. The whole point of the exercise was for someone to try to reach a joint of meat tied to the top. 'Many tried, but no one ever got to the top,' said Ned, 'and after a couple of months the pole was taken down and chopped-up for firewood.' The picture and story came to us via *The Huntsman*, house magazine of Joshua Tetley & Son.

Across the road from another White Cross – at Guiseley – is 'the most famous fish and chip shop in the world'. Such a claim comes easily to those who live in the county they often refer to as 'the Texas of England.' And whatever the good folks of Guiseley might say, Leeds 'Loiners' regard Harry Ramsden's as a pan of their city. It all started in a small way, of course – in this well-preserved wooden hut in which Harry established his business on 20 December 1928.

Nah, then... there is them 'at knows it an' them 'ats ignorant that a Yorkshireman's motto is (cut down to the vital bit): 'If tha' ivver does owt for nowt, allus do it for thissen,' Well, summat for nowt attracted thousands of 'thissens' to Guiseley on a day in 1951 when Harry decided to mark his success and reward the first 8,000 customers in the queue with fish 'n chip portions costing the equivalent of 2p. How they sorted out the queue, pictured here, remains a mystery but in the event everyone had a great day out.

It was early next morning before the multitude was served and Harry is seen here (on right with wing collar), having his hand shaken as frying finished at 2am.

Harry Ramsden's continued to grow and grow and as visitors came from all parts of the world to swell the ranks of Yorkshire customers, its fame spread and requests that Harry Ramsden-style restaurants be set up in other countries have been met. Meanwhile, the home base expanded and has long outgrown the premises as depicted in this January 1964 picture. In fairness, mention should be made of at least one of several other fish shops in the area which achieved international fame. John Arlott, the famous cricket commentator, was one of many international media representatives who traditionally went to Brett's, in Headingley, Leeds, when they were covering Test matches. He put the cat among the pigeons, or fish 'n chips, when he wrote a much-quoted piece in a national newspaper, making various complimentary remarks about Brett's and adding '...the best fish and chip shops in the world are within 11 miles of Bradford Town Hall'. Well, there were then over 300 chip shops in the Leeds area alone, but no doubt John had weighed-up things carefully before trailing this fishy bit across Yorkshire bows. Chip shop owners and customers all over Leeds and Bradford (whose city rivalries are ancient and still lasting', poured over maps with rulers, bits of strong string and spanned fingers to see if their premises were on the hallowed ground. Owners of the best-known Leeds establishments were pleased, or relieved, to declare that 'as the crow flies' they were within the distance...even if it meant stretching a (fisherman's) line a little.

Out of one uniform and into another. Quite a few boiled shirts and 'dicky bows' among these members of Leeds Transpon Department's Male Voice Choir. They were singing at a Remembrance Day concert in 1936 at the Paramount Cinema in The Headrow. The film that week was *Little Lord Fauntleroy* starring Freddie Banholomew.

Between the wars, a far-sighted builder saw that the Otley Road out of Leeds would become a major artery for travellers to and from the city. So, handy for Golden Acre Park (a picture of which appears in the Lungs of a City section), and within 20 minutes of the city centre in those days, he built the Parkway Hotel (now the Jarvis Parkway) between Lawnswood and Bramhope. A splendid establishment with well-laid-out public rooms and bars, it had bedrooms with facilities as far ahead of its many contemporaries as was the average American motel ahead of what went for motels in Britain in 1949. And thereby lay the next move onward, for a visit to the US by its proprietor led to the idea of giving the place a Hollywood atmosphere and there soon emerged the Coconut Grove nightclub in a ballroom complete with imitation palm trees and murals of Hawaiian beaches. The Rileys and MGs of young bloods from all over north Leeds and beyond poured in and lissom lasses from the avenues of Moortown, Roundhay, Adel and the rising up-market villages down in the Wharfe Valley could close their eyes and imagine they were dancing with Clark Gable, Robert Taylor or Cary Grant. What their partners had in mind is a matter of conjecture. Pictures: Collection of the late Mr C.B. Bairstow.

The train of thought that led to the night club also produced the idea of a FIorida-style lido near the hotel and soon the Blue Lagoon was attracting big crowds. Males with 'short-back-and-side' haircuts, or greased and 'slarted back a la Clark Gable, mingled with females in bathing costumes containing enough material in a single garment to equip a platoon of formation swimmers in years to come. These two pictures say it all. Collection of the late Mr C.B. Bairstow.

Meaniwhile, across the city at the bottom of Roundhay Park there was this pool, popular with small fry over the years. Mums and dads could park their prams, take a deckchair, then unload the children into the paddling pool, shown here in this July 1955 picture.

Have the US Cavalry landed? Or is it the Royal Canadian Mounted Police? Or have the Aussies arrived in Austhorpe? All wrong. It is the 25th North-West Leeds Methodist Scout Troop on a White Rose Motors outing at Rhyl in 1923. Mr W. Forrest, of Leafield Close, Leeds 17, who supplied the picture, has pointed out his position in the corner of the back seat.

THE SLUMS OF LEEDS

Take a stranger on a tour of Leeds, drive out along Clay Pit Lane and down the Sheepscar Link Road through Little London and, especially if they are from abroad, it is 10 to one he or she will express surprise at the ordered ranks of terrace houses, rising like some great red-brick parade up through the Bayswaters to the Conways, the Lascelles to the Luxors, where Roundhay Road climbs toward Harehills. 'Is that where the workers live? some will ask.

Well, all sorts of people live there, but compared with some areas where the workers used to live, these red-brick terraces are little palaces.

The slum areas of Leeds, some of which went back several hundred years, were squeezed into the nooks and crannies of the central area, then burst out into what would later be known as the inner suburbs. The influx of labour from countryside to city, and the conditions prevailing, meant that few of the people seeking a better life were any better off than they had been in tumbledown country cottages. There was little planning and a lot more people, so that conditions generally were often appalling as the city developed in the 19th century. As the turn of the century approached, the local authority simply had to take action and both they and private developers began to do something about conditions unimaginable to the majority of people under the age of 40 today.

Compulsory clearances were made as far back as the 1870s, and although an Act of Parliament in the early 1900s ruled that 'back-to-backs' which had replaced many of the original slums should no longer be built, a loophole meant that in Leeds builders were still putting them up into the 1930s. But they were fairly popular, creating a community spirit that would generally be lost with the coming of council housing estates.

The horrors of open drains, shared outside lavatories, a mix of uneven stone flags and cobblestones, industrial premises over the wall and some families living in what were little more than cellars are self-evident in this shot of an unnamed back yard. Even so, its residents kept it tidier than streets in the worst slums of Leeds – perhaps even more so than some areas today.

In times when errant youngsters 'had nothing to do' (an oft-heard phrase today), they were quickly found something to keep them occupied and a chalked notice 'Errand Boys Rest' on the wall end here shows one way of keeping idle hands busy, long before 'trainee couch potato' tripped lightly from the lips of parents in the western world. Mrs M. Dodds, of Lynwood Crescent, Leeds, sent us this picture of Little Woodhouse Street (she used to live in the second house down).

Though a cut above the city's worst slums, the area soon started to deteriorate as factories and workshops mingled with the houses on the right. The Clarendon Wing of Leeds Infirmary now stands on the site.

Escape from the slums and other areas for over 3,000 Loiners came with the development of Quarry Hill Flats – the largest block in Europe, the site of which is now occupied by Quarry House, the controversially plush headquarters of the Department of Social Security – more generally known as the 'Russian Space Station' or 'Chinese Embassy'.

It certainly offends many a critical eye observing it down The Headrow. But our picture shows its predecessor under construction in the mid-1930s. The occupants of the flats were almost 'like villagers in a city' according to some of them. Had they survived until the 1980s or 1990s, it is likely that someone would have based a TV soap opera on them for their stories were legion, ranging from

murders to 'flashers', horror stories of what had been put down their unusual waste disposal sinks and a laundry big enough to service several regiments. But the horror stories were in the minority. Most residents liked the flats, give or take the odd whinge, and they were streets ahead of what many had been used to in the past.

The first section of Quarry Hill opened in 1938 and eventually there were 938 individual homes in the block. But within 25 years the gritty Leeds atmosphere had done its worst, and this March 1963 shot shows one of the largest sections hidden behind a huge plastic screen. It had 2,600 one-yard-wide pieces, making a total covering well over four miles in length. Behind the screen, workmen were busy renovating the outside walls of Quarry Hill. But however good the repairs, the economics of running such a huge block were not to prove viable in the long (or more accurately short) run, so that their rise and fall came within a half century.

Meanwhile, the re-housing drive continued and although the slum menace had declined, people's aspirations had risen. As more terraces and back-to-backs came up for clearance, there were blips in the system as residents due to be moved sometimes became isolated in vandalised streets of empty homes while they waited for suitable council houses to be allocated. In the 1960s, the *Yorkshire Evening Post* was moved to run a number of stories on the problem and in this photograph, Councillor Mrs May Sexton chats with two young boys near a still-occupied home amid the growing dereliction of the rest of the street.

SPORTING LEEDS

Soccer

Sportsman, businessman, Don Revie, pictured later in his career when he had branchcd out into the commercial field. But he never lost that sporting touch.

England centre-half 'Big Jack' Charlton, brother of fellow international Bobby, was also into business, looking the real 'city gent' as he posed outside a shop bearing his name. One of the biggest and most popular names in football, Jack never lost his head in the clouds – he can still find the time to take his grandchildren for a walk in the Leeds suburb where they live.

Jack's size (second from left) is clcar in this picture where the team is 'stepped down to Scottish international Billy Bremner on the extreme right.

By 1962 Welsh international John Charles – better known as 'Big John' to the fans – was more famous than the American pop song of that title.

Bobby Collins of Scotland achieves a near-vertical take-off during a training session at Elland Road.
caption

The then Lord Mayor, Alderman John Raffeny, saw fit to wave his crutch with excitement as he welcomed the Leeds team to a Civic Reception after they won the European Fairs Cup in 1968. Behind him are some of the many guests on the steps of the Civic Hall.

...And when Billy Bremner raised the trophy the fans went wild. They 'supped some stiff' in Leeds that night!

Here is another great line-up of famous faces as the team poses with the Football League Championship trophy which they won in 1970.

United fans were up good and early to seethe sights in London when their team met Chelsea in the FA Cup Final at Wembley in 1970. It was a 2–2 draw amd Chelsea won the replay 2–1.

Cricket

Over the years, Leeds businessman Manny Cussins gave tremendous support to Leeds United. He was chairman during many of the 'Glory Years'.

Former Yorkshire and England cricketer Bill Bowes brought an expertise to cricket writing in the *Yorkshire Evening Post* that made his column a 'must' for sports fans among its readers.

Had there been a match and a good crowd, it would have been 'just as well it's a fine day' for those on the wide open terraces at Headingley in 1897.

Many years on and it is a more typical Headingley day, with overcoats on and collars turned lip against a stiff breeze. But, for a Yorkshireman, especially if he is from Leeds, it is still getting near to heaven...especially if England (or, maybe better still, Yorkshire) are winning.

Maurice Leyland does up his pads at Headingley in 1938.

An absolute gentleman in everyday life, and a 'gentle giant' to many on the cricket field, Bill Bowes was, nevertheless, a formidable figure as a bowler. It was once estimated that, at the top of the curve of his bowling action, the ball left his hand at over 9ft above the ground.

On their way to check the wicket, captains Don Bradman and Norman Yardley stride out applauded by obviously adoring fans on the hallowed turf in 1948.

Left: The 'Old Enemy' – but ever welcome – Don Bradman gets a pat from a schoolboy as he goes out to bat for Australia. *Right:* Wilf Barber (left) and Len Hutton stroll out to slog it out in a 1946 Yorkshire v Hampshire match.

Left: Herbert's Sutcliffe's boots were well and truly spiked as he marched on to the field to get a slice of the action. *Right:* 'Nah then, it is like this...' Brian Close and Freddie Trueman sizing things up at the nets.

Wearing his sleeve in a style in 1961 that most youngsters seem to have adopted today, Ray Illingworth at practise at Headingley.

Rugby League

A postcard showing the Leeds (Rugby) Football Club team before their match with Keighley in 1908.

The Lord Mayor of Leeds being introduced to the Leeds team before their match with Hunslet in the Northern Rugby League Championship Final at Elland Road in April 1938. Hunslet won 8–2 before a crowd of 54,112.

When men were men – there were no thoughts of summer matches whcn Leeds RL full-back Bev Risman joined the attack and slipped a reverse pass to John Langley on the snow-covered pitch at Headingley in February 1969. Curiously, the under-pitch electric heating was said to have been switched on. The Leeds team went to their 17th successive win of the season, by 29–4, against Halifax.

Exultation by Leeds fans as they surge on to the field to chair skipper Lewis Jones to the stand to receive the trophy after a memorable Northern Rugby League Championship Final at Odsal in May 1961. It was the first time Leeds had won the trophy.

It was certainly just as well that there was no February cricket at Parkside in 1958. The pitch and pavillion were flooded and it needed assistance from the Leeds Fire Brigade to pump the place dry. Fortunately, the Hunslet RL club's ground was not seriously affected and they were able to play St Helen's the same afternoon.

Not exactly your 'Superdome' scene – the Middleton end of the Parkside ground was known by most fans as 'Mother Benson's' because a lady of that name had the old cottages there before the RL ground was laid out. But in November 1956, they were under threat because the club planned a redevelopment which included a 'Spion Kop' to house 12,000 in place of the cottages.

By 1959, the cottages had gone and these chaps were clearing the terraces at Mother Benson's end to make a larger playing area. Volunteers did the preliminary work, then a bulldozer moved in to push the banking back to where the cottages used to stand. Mr Sam Longbottom, in the centre, had been a Hunslet fan since he was a boy and was there for the Four Cup victory celebrations in 1908.

Hunslet's Tommy Thompson makes a fine attempt to score as Dewsbury full-back Bob Hirst flings himself into the tackle during an August 1966 game at Parkside. Thompson made the line but the referee ruled that he did not ground the ball correctly.

A bitter end – all gone – but not forgotten. A lonely fan surveys the empty Parkside ground a few days after Hunslet RL played their last match there in 1973.

We leave Headingley as we started – cold. It was raincoats, not anoraks, on just about every back as England took on India. No doubt the latter team's players could justly say they did not feel much at home on such a dismal day. The picture is undated, but considering the many 'short back and sides' haircuts, and chaps wearing ex-army berets, it looks like an early post-World War Two match. The Indians toured in 1952, so perhaps it was then.

WARTIME LEEDS

Although Leeds suffered nothing like the destruction wrought by the German bombing of two other Yorkshire cities – Sheffield and Hull – it did have its attacks and many homes and several public buildings were damaged in addition to industrial and commercial premises,

Some say that what saved the city was the very pollution which came to be so heavily-criticised in later years, There is evidence that Kirkstall Forge, which would have been a prime target, escaped much attention from the Luftwaffe because its bomber crews had difficulty in identifying targets in the fog, haze, and smoke-prone Aire valley.

They did manage to hit some important industrial targets in the Hunslet and south Leeds areas, and there was some suspicion of collaboration; or that the bombers used photographs gathered on pre-war passes by German airships; or immediately before the war reconnaissance flights by Luftwaffe aircraft which certainly carried out such work along the Yorkshire and North-East coastlines,

The collaboration theory arose when a well-known Leeds local authority official returned from military service with maps he found in the drawer of a German headquarters desk after the Normandy landings. These 'Nord-Midland' maps, as they were known, included some of the Leeds area where railway lines and other features inside Hunslet factories were shown. Such information could not have been gained from aerial pictures,

In addition to the maps, the author has also seen Luftwaffe reconnaissance pictures of Leeds on which targets such as gas-holders – a favourite Luftwaffe target – are clearly marked,

This 'semi' was completely 'detached' by a bomb which fell on a Leeds suburb. All that remains of the right-hand house is the guttering which used to be over the front bedroom window.

The benefits of a corrugated metal 'Anderson' shelter dug into the garden)between the two ground-floor windows) are clear. What is left of the house on the left probably had to be demolished, cracks in the wall extend through to next door, but the shelter is intact. This was 1942, in Bramley.

The end of this row of terraced houses was ripped wide open in a raid on the city.

The York Road area of the city suffered more damage than many other districts. Of these two older houses, the one on the left was completely wrecked – the bath and sink of the one on the right hang perilously over the living room. The 'new' chimney is a tribute to whoever built it! As for the garden, the only thing left worthy of the description is a square yard of privet hedge in the foreground.

Anyone old enough to recall the days of air raids will immediately think of one famous phrase on seeing this picture: 'Put that light out!' Air-raid wardens Mr and Mrs E.M. Wright arc pictured complete with 'tin hats' and gas mask cases slung over their shoulders. Though the butt of many jokes, most wardens did a splendid job, often under arduous conditions. For younger readers: no lights were allowed to be seen from any premises during wartime, hence the famous remark which was usually uttered by air-raid wardens.

'Ello, Ello, Ello...wots this' ere then...?' Three stalwart policemen keep guard on the remains of a Luftwaffe Messerschmitt Bf109 displayed in City Square, much to the satisfaction of a grandstand of small boys. The bullet-ripped fuselage bore testimony to the RAF's shooting, but whoever set-up the display appears to have put the wings back to front – or upside down,

King George VI (in uniform) and Queen Elizabeth (now Queen Elizabeth the Queen Mother) came to see the bomb damage in 1940. Someone kindly provided a chair – on the pavement outside a wrecked house – in case she wanted to sit down, but she graciously declined.

Smiling as ever, she was here again in March 1944, and visited the Leeds Blood Transfusion Service's wartime base, along with the King, who is in RAF uniform on the left.

And there were other famous visitors, both during and soon after the war. The crowds waited for it – and they got it – Prime Minister Winston Churchill gives the famous 'V' sign as he and Mrs Churchill, his 'beloved Clementine' leave Leeds Civic Hall.

Weather-wise, it was not the best of days when General Charles de Gaulle came to the city in February 1942, to give his support to Leeds Warship Week, which raised cash for the *Ark Royal* and established a strong link with the Royal Navy which has continued over the years. Despite the weather, the Free French leader was given a warm welcome and you have our assurance that he is on that podium where, in true Navy style, the signal was 'Save'.

The workers of Leeds made a tremendous contribution to the nation's war effort. Here is just a small sample of tanks turned out by the Royal Ordnance Factory at Barnbow. As soon as the trains were loaded, the tanks would be on their way to 'holding' areas or straight into action.

The most publicised – though not at the time – wartime production plant on the area was the Ministry of Aircraft Production 'shadow factory' at Yeadon, better known to everyone as 'Avro's' because it was aircraft of A.V. Roe that were built there. Hundreds of Lancaster bombers and other Avro types such as the Anson and York made their first flights from Yeadon and the whole story has been no better told than in *Mother Worked at Avro* by Gerald Myers, who kindly gave me permission to use these pictures from the book. This one, via Mrs Doreen Varley, of Bradford, shows the last Lancaster (TX 273), Anson (PH 315) and York built at the factory, with hundreds of employees on 18 October 1945. Mrs Varley had worked there on wire-splicing and Anson wing assembly.

Mr Ray Marshall gave permission to use this photograph of some of those involved in the final inspcction and test-flying of Yeadon-built aircraft, Captain Worrall, the airport controller and chief test pilot, is third from the right – immediately behind the ladies in the front row. As recorded in the Planes section, it was his chance remark which led to the whole Yeadon project.

Some of the York and Lancaster final assembly personnel pictured in 1945. Among them is Mr Alfred Harris who supplied the photograph.

Oh, the memory, and the smell! – of the Leeds Civic Restaurant, opened in the bowels of Leeds Town Hall in 1942. Long after the war, judges in the building's courts are said to have complained about it. Journalists covering long court cases have been known to go out and make two laps of the building to get some fresh air...but the restaurant was not all that bad. And where else could you get a lunch of roast beef, two veg, pudding, bread and butter and coffee for one shilling? Perhaps, after all, it was an 'aroma', not a smell!

While on the subject of smells – in common with bus companies all over the country, the West Yorkshire set out to beat the petrol shortage in World War Two by equipping many vehicles with gas producers mounted on trailers. Conductors would jump off at various stops to 'poke about' in the Heath Robinson-like contraption. Passengers (and more particularly following motorists) remember it for the stench it produced.

'You caused the damage – now you can get cracking on putting it right again,' might well have been the attitude of the foreman on this Farsley building site as German POWs (prisoners-of-war) were put to work on road building.

Up to this point, the citizens of Leeds had not been over-enthusiastic about anything that might be said by a German admiral, but they literally mobbed this *Yorkshire Evening Post* seller for news of Doenitz's announcement of the German surrender.

And then it was all over. The Sergeant Major would have cried if he'd seen 'em. Two corporals and a young RAF type enter into the spirit of things with the VE Day revellers in Albion Street in 1945.

Cooks, bottle washers, messenger boys, ATS girls, shop assistants, office workers – they were all letting their hair down outside the NAAFI club in Albion Street on VE Day.

Sailors have all the luck! This one was the centre of attention from a crowd of ATS girls in Albion Street.

It rained heavily during celebrations in Leeds – but there is hardly a single person in the huge crowd outside the Town Hall who did not have a smile.

The scene in The Headrow, with a column of Servicemen and their vehicles stretching as far as the eye can see. The salute was taken on the steps of thc Town Hall and thousands of 'Loiners' turned out for the occasion.

'Welcome Home' says the banner over the middle of the street. There are V-signs painted on the wall of every house and a giant 'V' adorns the cobblestones as grandmothers, mothers and relations parade 'the kids' in preparation for a war's end party in this Leeds street. The two lads on the right look as though they have just been de-mobbed, and sticky brown paper crosses still adorn the house windows to prevent flying glass in the event of air raids.

The lasses in this Kirkstall factory posed for the photographer in their decorated workroom as they hurried through their shift in preparation for a VE Day party.

Here is another party, 'down the backs', with a tarpaulin rigged as an improvised shelter. Everyone – other than the baby in the high chair – knew how to give the 'V' sign, though no doubt she might pick it up in later years.

Manor Grove, Leeds, might have been a long way from Japan, but the folks who lived there were determined to show their appreciation of what 'our lads and lasses' in the Pacific war zone had done to bring them to the point of a VJ Day party. Note the street's air raid shelters on the right.

And finally, it was all over. Soldiers on leave join the neighbours in a VJ party in Hillcrest Avenue, Leeds, with a accompaniment (on the left) for the dancers.

No.609 (West Riding) Squadron, Auxiliary Air Force (later to have the word Royal added before the Auxiliary), was formed at Yeadon on 10 February 1936. It was then assumed that one of its tasks would be the defence of West Riding cities and towns 'if war came'. When it did, 609 had an outstanding record throughout, and not least in the Battle of Britain when it was equipped with Spitfires. Its first commanding officer was S/Ldr Harald Peake (who became chairman of Lloyd's Bank in post-war years). Its eighth, and youngest CO, at 22, was R.P. 'Bee' Beamont, DSO, DFC & Bar, credited with spearheading 609's efforts to make the Hawker Typhoon one of the hardest-hitting and most successful fighter-bombers of World War Two. He went on to become one of the world's top test pilots.

Some of the squadron's Yorkshire members served with it for almost the whole of the war, but it also embraced pilots from over a dozen other countries, including Australia, Belgium, Canada, Poland and South Africa. Many of them keep in touch via the squadron's Association which has its own dedicated 609 Memorial Room at the Yorkshire Air Museum at Elvington, near York. Among those early members was 'Darkie' Hanson MBE who, as a Flight Lieutenant, became its Engineering Officer. He lives within the sound of a six-hit at Headingley cricket ground.

After the war, by which time the squadron was equipped with Meteor jets, it moved from Yeadon to Church Fenton where it finally disbanded in 1957. During the 1950s it had a Town Headquarters at Wheatfields, Headingley, now a renowned hospice, which has received much support from *Yorkshire Evening Post* readers via the newspaper's 'Half and Half' appeal. It was there that this photograph was taken in the mid-1950s. Among those pictured are, front row (left to right): Darkie Hanson, Flt/Lt Doug Thomas (Training Officer), S/Ldr Dave Shaw (609's last CO), Flt/Lt 'Mac' McConnell (Accounts Officer) and Pilot Officer Andy McAlpine. Among those standing are: Flt/Lt Pete Hodgson (extreme left), and Flt/Lt 'Doc' Lawrence (Medical Officer) in check waistcoat. On the extreme right is Flt/Lt Pete Bailey (Intelligence Officer), next to him (in dark tie) is Flt/Lt Steve Lerche, who became a civil pilot, and Flt/Lt Frank Reacroft (behind 'Mac' McConnell) a 609 pilot who was later with Heaps Tours in Leeds.

YORKSHIRE EVENING POST
– *a Newspaper for all times*

Newspapers are in a sense transient. Their immediate relevance is to the day of publication. But in another sense their development over the years keeps pace with the growth of the community which they serve and gives them purpose, character and continuity.

The part the *Yorkshire Evening Post* has played in that process is linked directly to forebears that go back to 2 July 1754, when Griffith Wright printed the first issue of the *Leedes Intelligencer.* Wright's paper, a weekly, chronicled the Industrial Revolution and sharpened itself by competing with a rival called the *Leeds Mercury* (founded 1718).

Its transformation to a daily came in 1866 when a newly-formed company, the Yorkshire Conservative Newspaper Co Ltd, turned the *Intelligencer* into the *Yorkshire Post*. By 1923, the battle with the *Leeds Mercury* was over and it was acquired by the YCN company and provided with a new editor, William Linton Andrews, who was knighted in 1954. The two papers continued separate publication for 16 years but were merged in 1939, mainly because of wartime newsprint restrictions. The two 'grand old titles' had, since September 1890, had a young and vigorous companion in the shape of the *Yorkshire Evening Post*. During its 106 years it has thrown roots deep into the community, especially in the city of Leeds.

Developments in the city, including a rapidly increasing growth in city-centre traffic, plus a need to incorporate complex advances in almost every aspect of newspaper production, led to a decision in the early 1960s to find new premises.

Mr Gordon Linacre was briefed accordingly when he was appointed Managing Director in April 1965, and from that time the days of the curious rabbit warren known affectionately as 'the old lady of Albion Street' were numbered.

Subsequently, the company was retitled *Yorkshire Post* Newspapers Limited and a site in Wellington Street was acquired from the Corporation in October 1967. Once building started, progress was such that on 30 October 1969, the late Sir Kenneth Parkinson, then Chairman, was able to perform the topping-out ceremony.

The paper's newspaper sellers were quickly ready for the 'off' when from South Africa came one of the biggest stories since the paper was launched, and the bills proclaimed: 'Ladysmith Relieved – National Rejoicing'. Near-identical bills were rushed out by every daily newspaper in the land on receipt of the news from the Boer War zone (1899–1902).

The move from Albion Street to the new premises came in a carefully planned and co-ordinated operation on the weekend of 26–27 September 1970. It began immediately after the printing of the Saturday night's *Yorkshire Evening Post* and was achieved in time for both papers to be printed at Wellington Street on the Monday. Prince Charles carried-out the official opening of the new building in December of the following year.

In November 1983, Sir Kenneth was succeeded as Chairman by Gordon Linacre, who was himself knighted in 1986. He continued to play a leading role into the development of the Company until he retired as Chairman and was made President in September 1990.

Today, the *Yorkshire Post* Newspapers Building houses one of the most advanced newspaper publishing organisations in Europe.

Although many newspaper sellers' barrows were retained for years for city-centre use, the company invested early in motor transport and this publicity picture, entitled 'An early gogetter' shows one of the balloon-tyred vans used to take newspapers to all parts of the *YEP*'s rapidly-increasing circulation area.

Meanwhile, the newspaper seller's voice was his best selling medium and here is a group in full cry as they rush freshly-printed copies out of the Basinghall Street 'loading bay' at the rear of the paper's long-time Albion Street headquarters. Or, on reflection, were they shouting the odds for that day's runners on the 'Sporting Special' bill fastened to the gate?

Efforts in aid of various good causes have been spear-headed, or launched and run by the *Yorkshire Evening Post* practically throughout its lifetime – and have raised millions of pounds in the process. The 'Boots for the Bairns' campaign raised money to provide footwear for thousands of children living in the city's slums. The annual Christmas Fund and Toy Appeal for which the late Geoffrey Halton (once the paper's famous motoring correspondent and later a member of the publicity staff) was a tireless worker, brought in large sums of cash to provide toys for children of the poor and this picture shows food parcels being prepared to provide Christmas Cheer for those in poor homes in December 1934.

Scores of Leeds area pubs and various organisations ran regular events to support the Toy Appeal. Today they, and thousands of individual readers have given donations to the 'Half and Half' Appeal in aid of local hospices.

Another member of the publicity staff in the 1930s was Richard Pape, seen here with the paper's loudspeaker van which toured galas, fétes and local shows. It bore the words 'The Original Buff' on

its sides, referring to the colour of the newsprint in use in those days. Richard later produced a book *Boldness He My Friend* as a result of his wartime experiences, particularly as a prisoner-of-war.

It is 10.30am and a reasonably pleasant morning, judging by the ladies' dresses. The geraniums are flowering in the window boxes above what was, for years, the 'front counter' area of the then Yorkshire Conservative Newspaper Company's offices in Albion Street. *Yorkshire Post* signs were well in evidence and some bills in the windows reveal that the *Yorkshire Evening Post* was also in business perhaps confirming the rivalry that existed between some areas of the two newspapers. And a sign of things to come – Albion Place was already a one-way street, according to the 'No right turn' sign on the vintage traffic light in the bottom corner.

Looking down Albion Street from offices on the corner of Albion Place, across from the veteran 'Belisha beacon' in the bottom left-hand corner. The YCN company occupied all the property from

the corner of Commercial Street up to the staunchly pillared doorway of Martin's the cleaners, on the right, plus a hotch-potch of around a dozen other buildings which ran from behind this block through to Basinghall Street. Above the larger of the two archways near the centre of the picture (commonly known as 'the bow way') is a stone relief sign reading '*The Yorkshire Post*'. Along to the right, next to the top of Martin's entrance, another reading 1754. It was a fine façade, with some splendid ironwork: behind each pillar in the smaller entrance to the right of the main arch the name '*Yorkshire Post*' was cast. When the property was demolished following the company's move to Wellington Street, among the items 'rescued', to reappear in the new office of the late John Edwards, then Editor of the *Yorkshire Post*, were the two castings. They deserved to be there.

The *Yorkshire Evening Post* Women's Circle, which became one of the largest organisations of its type in Britain, was launched on 7 July 1970 by Mr Ewart Clay, then Editor of the newspaper, in company with the author. All manner of functions were organised for women readers who joined in their thousands. 'It's the best thing that ever happened for women in Leeds,' said a waitress at a Queen's Hotel business function, when a top table speaker asked what the Circle was all about. A popular event was the annual Christmas get together – to which husbands or boyfriends could be invited. This one was at the Windmill Hotel, Seacroft. But the activity which really made the Circle's name was its holiday programme. Originally, all the holidays were escorted, and this gave a satisfaction and security which meant that ladies could travel alone, for they always made friends on the trips. The first 'overseas' holiday was to Majorca, and it received extensive coverage in the Spanish Press. But soon women who had never been any further than Blackpool or Bridlington were visiting America, Canada, South Africa, and many other destinations. The second picture was taken on the occasion of the first Women's Circle trip to the Far East. Sandra Reed, who was the Circle's organiser then is in the striped dress, ninth from the right.